Tim Chester

Matthew

Kingdom Treasure

GOOD BOOK GUIDE

9-Session Bible Study

Matthew For You

These studies are adapted from *Matthew For You*. If you are reading *Matthew For You* alongside this Good Book Guide, here is how the studies in this booklet link to the chapters of *Matthew For You*:

Study 1 > Ch 1
Study 2 > Ch 2
Study 3 > Ch 3-4
Study 4 > Ch 5-6
Study 5 > Ch 7
Study 6 > Ch 8
Study 7 > Ch 10-11
Study 8 > Ch 13
Study 9 > Ch 14

Find out more about *Matthew For You* at:
www.thegoodbook.com/for-you

Matthew: Kingdom Treasure
A Good Book Guide

Published by The Good Book Company

thegoodbook.com | thegoodbook.co.uk
thegoodbook.com.au | thegoodbook.co.nz

A CIP catalogue record for this book is available from the British Library.

Design by André Parker and Drew McCall

ISBN: 9781784984977 | JOB-008372 | Printed in Turkey

Contents

Introduction 4

Why Study Matthew? 5

1. The Promised One 7
   Matthew 1:1 – 2:12

2. The King Wins for Us 15
   Matthew 3:1 – 4:11

3. The Renewed Life 21
   Matthew 5:1-12, 17-48

4. The King's Authority 29
   Matthew 8:23 – 9:8; 10:1-31

5. The Kingdom Resisted 35
   Matthew 12:1-14; 13:24-46

6. Peter's Hits and Misses 41
   Matthew 14:22-36; 16:13-28

7. The First, Last and the Last, First 47
   Matthew 20:1-16; 21:1-32

8. The Death of the King 53
   Matthew 26:31-56; 27:32-54

9. The King Lives 59
   Matthew 28:1-10, 16-20

Leader's Guide 65

Introduction

One of the Bible writers described God's word as "a lamp for my feet, a light on my path" (Psalm 119:105, NIV). God gave us the Bible to tell us about who he is and what he wants for us. He speaks through it by his Spirit and lights our way through life.

That means that we need to look carefully at the Bible and uncover its meaning—but we also need to apply what we've discovered to our lives.

Good Book Guides are designed to help you do just that. The sessions in this book are interactive and easy to lead. They're perfect for use in groups or for personal study.

Let's take a look at what is included in each session.

Talkabout: Every session starts with an ice-breaker question, designed to get people talking around a subject that links to the Bible study.

Investigate: These questions help you explore what the passage is about.

Apply: These questions are designed to get you thinking practically: what does this Bible teaching mean for you and your church?

Explore More: These optional sections help you to go deeper or to explore another part of the Bible which connects with the main passage.

Getting Personal: These sections are a chance for personal reflection. Some groups may feel comfortable discussing these, but you may prefer to look at them quietly as individuals instead—or leave them out.

Pray: Here, you're invited to pray in the light of the truths and challenges you've seen in the study.

Each session is also designed to be easily split into two! Watch out for the **Apply** section that comes halfway through, and stop there if you haven't got time to do the whole thing in one go.

In the back of the book, you'll find a **Leader's Guide**, which provides helpful notes on every question, along with everything else that group leaders need in order to facilitate a great session and help the group uncover the riches of God's light-giving word.

Why Study Matthew?

Matthew's Gospel tells the story of Jesus—Immanuel, God with us, Israel's Messiah and the hope of all nations. Whether you're a Jew or a Gentile, this is the story of your Saviour-King. Matthew's Gospel is something of a training manual to show you how you can and should live within this wonderful story.

"Every teacher of the law who has become a disciple in the kingdom of heaven is like the owner of a house who brings out of his storeroom new treasures as well as old." So says Jesus in Matthew 13:52. It's a saying only Matthew includes, and it's likely that he saw it as a description of himself. Matthew is a teacher of the law who has become a disciple of Jesus (or a disciple who has become a teacher of the law). And his Gospel brings new treasures out from the storehouse of Scripture. In other words, Matthew shows how Jesus fulfils the Old Testament.

Matthew's concern to be a teacher of the law is also reflected in the amount of the teaching of Jesus that he includes. Matthew often trims down stories by leaving out details that Mark and Luke cover and instead includes teaching that Mark and Luke leave out. This focus on teaching is also reflected in the structure of the Gospel. In addition to its introduction (1 – 2) and climax (26 – 28), Matthew has five main sections that are divided up with a phrase along the lines of "When Jesus had finished saying these things..." (7:28-29, and see similar in 11:1, 13:53, 19:1, 26:1).

It's widely thought that in the first instance Matthew wrote for Jewish believers or maybe Jewish seekers—that may be one reason for his emphasis on Jesus as the fulfilment of the Old Testament. Yet despite this, Matthew also portrays Jesus as sent for all nations.

Jesus is our Saviour and King. His miracles show him to be God's King with the authority to establish God's kingdom and to be God's Saviour with the power to save God's people. Yet, ultimately, Jesus proves to be the King who saves by dying in our place and rising again to give us life.

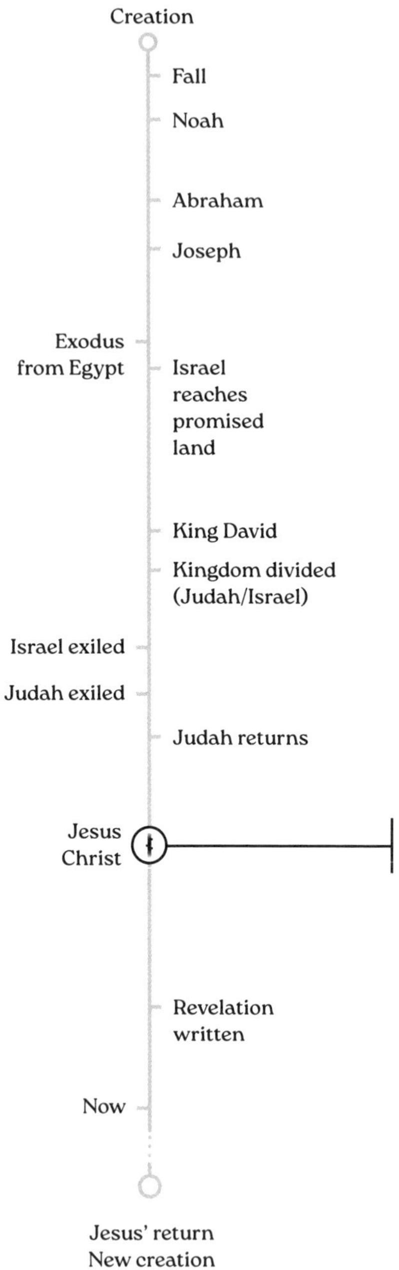

Matthew

1st century AD

1

The Promised One

Matthew 1:1 - 2:12

Talkabout

1. Imagine you were going to introduce another member of your group to someone they didn't know (at a party or after church, or similar). What would you say about them by way of introduction?

In the opening of Matthew's Gospel, he introduces us to his chief subject (who is also his friend): "Jesus the Messiah" (1:1). Right out of the blocks, we discover some extraordinary claims about who Jesus is.

Investigate

Read Matthew 1:1-17

DICTIONARY

Messiah (v 1): the all-powerful, eternal King promised throughout the Old Testament.

For Matthew's Jewish readers, this list of names would have evoked a succession of stories from their history, all of which are about to find their fulfilment in Mary's child (v 17-18).

2. Matthew orders his genealogy to focus on three moments in particular from Israel's history. What are they (v 17)?

Let's consider each of those in turn.

Way back in Genesis 3, when humanity rejected God, we became enemies of God, and we live in a world under God's curse (Genesis 3).

3. Read Genesis 12:1-3. What does the connection with Abraham in Matthew 1 show us about what Jesus is going to do?

4. Read God's words to King David in 2 Samuel 7:11b-16. What does the connection with David in Matthew 1 show us about what Jesus is going to do?

    - Why might this have looked unlikely to readers in Matthew's day, living under the Roman Empire?

The third moment spotlighted in Matthew 1 is Israel's Exile to Babylon—which happened as God's judgment on their sin (v 12). In time, Ezra and Nehemiah led the people back to the land, but they still weren't truly free (Nehemiah 9:36-37).

5. In what way is the Exile from Babylon a picture of all of humanity's plight?

   - What does this connection with the Exile to Babylon tell us about what Jesus is going to do?

6. What point do you think Matthew is making by the particular women he chooses to include (v 3, 5, 6)? (For more information, see Genesis 34; Joshua 2; Ruth 1 – 4; 2 Samuel 11)

Getting Personal | OPTIONAL

The women named in Matthew 1 spotlight the fact that Jesus came to save Jews and Gentiles, men and women, sinners and sinned-against. "If the Lord Jesus was not ashamed to be born of a woman whose pedigree contained such names as those we have read today," said the 19th-century bishop J. C. Ryle, "we need not think that he will be ashamed to call us brethren, and to give us eternal life" (*Expository Thoughts on the Gospels*, p. 4).

Jesus is not ashamed to have you in his family. Are there particular corners of your heart where that sets you free?

Apply

We've seen that Jesus is the Son of Abraham come to reverse the curse to bring God's blessing; the promised King whose rule will set us free; and the one who will lead us home to God from exile.

7. What will happen in our hearts and lives if we lose sight of any one of these pictures of who Jesus is?

- Which of those pictures gives you the most comfort and reassurance in this moment, and why?

Investigate

📖 **Read Matthew 1:18-25**

DICTIONARY

The prophet (v 22): one of God's messengers in the Old Testament.

8. What do the two names given to Mary's child add to our understanding of who he is?

Explore More | OPTIONAL

Matthew 1:18-25 is the first of five stories surrounding the birth of Jesus, each of which contains a quote from the Old Testament (1:22-23; 2:6, 15, 17-18, 23). The first of these is from Isaiah 7.

📖 **Read Isaiah 7:1-17**

- What problem did Ahaz face (v 1-2)?

- What promise did God offer him (v 7-9)? What did Ahaz need to do in response (v 4)?

God even offered to give Ahaz a sign (v 10-11). But Ahaz refused to ask for one (v 12), opting instead for an alliance with Assyria (the rising superpower of the day). So God gave Ahaz a sign that Ahaz was not looking for.

- What was that sign (v 14)? And what would it point to (v 16-17)?

Ahaz thought he could do without God; but it was God who didn't need Ahaz. For God could bring the reign of David's sons to an end (as he did when Judah was exiled in Babylon) and then start afresh by raising up a new king from a virgin.

By quoting from Isaiah 7, Matthew draws together two lines of promise. First, God will raise up a new king from a virgin—a king who will trust God and restore God's rule. Second, God himself will come as Immanuel to save his people from their sins. These two trajectories converge in Mary's child. In his humanity, Jesus is the descendant of David; in his divinity, he is Immanuel: God with us.

How should we respond? By doing what Ahaz should have done: "Be careful, keep calm and don't be afraid" (v 4). Ahaz should have found confidence in the promises of God. He should have trusted the promise of a Saviour. And so should we.

Read Matthew 2:1-12

9. What different responses to the news of Jesus' birth do we see in this passage? Why do people respond in those ways?

- What is surprising about who responds in which way?

Getting Personal | OPTIONAL

God is infinite, unchanging, self-sustaining, eternal, invisible. He's not just a bigger version of us; he's utterly different. Yet there was a moment in history when he lay in a manger. If that's true, then the only sensible response is to join the Magi in worshipping Jesus.

10. How do we see God's promise to Abraham coming true in these verses?

Apply

11. There's a little bit of Herod in all of us. In what ways might people today be similarly "disturbed" by the idea of Jesus being King, and of having to submit to his rule? What about us?

    - What would it look like to respond like the Magi to Jesus instead?

12. If Jesus is King of all the nations, how should that shape our prayers, our finances and our churches?

Pray

Praise Jesus for all that he is: Son of Abraham, our true King, our way home, our Saviour, God with us, and the fulfilment of all his promises.

Ask for his help to live lives of wholehearted worship.

Pray that people from more and more nations would come to see Jesus as King.

2

The King Wins for Us

Matthew 3:1 - 4:11

The Story So Far…

Through Jesus' genealogy and the story of his birth, Matthew has introduced him as God's promised King—come to save people of all nations from their sin.

Talkabout

1. Imagine that a very important visitor is going to visit your community next week. How would you prepare?

Matthew introduces a new character in chapter 3: John the Baptist. He declares that God's kingdom is in the process of arriving—because, as we'll see, God's Messianic King is arriving. And it's time to get ready…

Investigate

📖 **Read Matthew 3:1-12**

DICTIONARY

Kingdom of heaven (v 2): life under Jesus Christ's perfect rule.
Winnowing fork (v 12): used by farmers to separate the wheat (the good part of the plant) from the chaff (which was thrown away or burned).

2. What does John tell people that they need to do to prepare for the coming kingdom (v 2)?

- What do the rest of these verses teach us about what that means or what it looks like?

3. John has come to prepare the people. But what will the one who comes after him do, according to verses 11-12? What do the images John uses mean, do you think?
    - Verse 11
    - Verse 12

Read Matthew 3:13-17

DICTIONARY

Fulfil all righteousness (v 15): obeying God's will.

4. Given what we've read in chapter 3 so far, what is surprising about verse 13?

5. Why does Jesus insist on being baptised? What does this mean, do you think?

Explore More | OPTIONAL

- Read the following verses describing figures in the Old Testament. How are they echoed in Matthew 3:13-17? What clues do they give us as to what is going on in this surprising incident?
    - The suffering servant: Isaiah 53:5, 12; 42:1
    - The anointed King: Psalm 2:7; 2 Samuel 7:12-14
    - Isaac, Abraham's son: Genesis 22:1-2

By being baptised, Jesus is obeying God's will ("fulfilling all righteousness", Matthew 3:15). How so?

The answer is in Isaiah's prophecy of a suffering servant who would redeem God's people by bearing their sin in their place: "He was pierced for our transgressions, he was crushed for our iniquities … and was numbered with the transgressors" (Isaiah 53:5, 12). In baptism Jesus identifies with his sinful people and so accepts the role of the suffering servant to which God has called him.

Apply

6. One day Jesus will return, axe and winnowing fork in hand, as it were, to enact this judgment. How can we prepare for this coming, according to these verses?

Getting Personal | OPTIONAL

The German Reformer Martin Luther once said, "When our Lord and Master Jesus Christ said, 'Repent' (Matthew 4:17), he willed the entire life of believers to be one of repentance".

Does repentance characterise your life as a believer? What was the last thing you repented of? Can you see ways in which you're producing fruit in keeping with repentance?

7. The image of Jesus "winnowing" grain points to how the coming of Jesus would divide 1st-century Judaism (3:7-12). It still divides humanity today, as the gospel is proclaimed and people either reject or accept it. How does this picture of Jesus put steel into our life and witness as his followers?

Investigate

The Old Testament imagery keeps coming in chapter 4. Here, Jesus is re-running the story of the people of Israel after the Exodus. Just as Israel was led by the pillars of cloud and fire to be tested in the wilderness for 40 years (Deuteronomy 8:2), so Jesus is led by the Spirit to be tested in the wilderness for 40 days (Matthew 4:1-2).

But chapter 4 also takes us back to an earlier test: the one in Genesis 3. Adam was the representative of humanity, and his failure became our failure. In his baptism, Jesus signalled that he was the representative of a new humanity. But would he succeed where Adam and Israel had failed?

Read Matthew 4:1-11

DICTIONARY

It is written (v 4): that is, written in the Jewish Scriptures (the Old Testament).

The holy city (v 5): Jerusalem.

8. Look at the three tests that Jesus undergoes. For each one, how does Satan subtly offer Jesus an opt-out of the suffering he must undergo as the suffering servant?
    - Test 1 (4:3-4; compare with 27:40)
    - Test 2 (4:5-7; compare with 26:51-54)
    - Test 3 (4:8-10)

9. What would the consequences have been if Jesus had said yes to any of Satan's offers? What was at stake?

Apply

10. Imagine a Christian friend tells you that they are trying (and often failing) to resist temptation in some area (e.g. watching pornography, yelling at their kids, grumbling about others behind their back). How could you use Matthew 3 and 4 to help and encourage them?

11. In what areas of your life do you need to hear the same help and encouragement?

Getting Personal | OPTIONAL

The great news of this passage is that I'm not simply left trying harder to be like Christ. I can rest assured that I've already passed the test in Christ. If I'm baptised into Christ, then God's verdict on Christ at his baptism becomes God's declaration to me: *You are my son, my daughter, whom I love; with you I am well pleased* (adapting Matthew 3:17).

Pause to imagine God saying those words to you right now.

Pray

Thank Jesus that he was willing to identify as one of us and that he passed the test that we could not.

Confess ways in which you've failed.

Rejoice that because of Jesus, you are nonetheless secure in your status as a son or daughter of God.

3

The Renewed Life

Matthew 5:1-12, 17-48

The Story So Far...

Through Jesus' genealogy and the story of his birth, Matthew has introduced him as God's promised King—come to save people of all nations from their sin.

Jesus was baptised by John to show his identification with sinful humanity; then he resisted Satan's temptations in the wilderness, passing the test on our behalf.

Talkabout

1. What is the secret to happiness? How do you think your non-Christian friends, family or co-workers would answer that question?

Investigate

Matthew 1 – 4 presents Jesus as the liberator who will end the exile through a new exodus. That theme continues in the first part of the Sermon on the Mount: the Beatitudes.

Read Matthew 5:1-12

DICTIONARY

Poor in spirit (v 3): broken.
Meek (v 5): humble, gentle.
Righteousness (v 6, 19): doing God's will.

2. Who is listening as Jesus delivers the "Sermon on the Mount" (v 1-2)? What might that tell us about how we should understand and apply this teaching today?

The word "blessed" means "happy" or "flourishing". The Beatitudes are not the entrance requirements of Christ's kingdom nor rewards for good behaviour. They're descriptions of how we can live a good life under Christ's kingship.

3. What do each of these descriptions have in common, would you say? (Look at the first half of each verse that begins "Blessed are...")

- Compare verses 3 and 10 with verses 4-9. What difference do you notice?

Getting Personal | OPTIONAL

Jesus gives his kingdom to people who feel their brokenness. Broken people receive his kingdom as a gift, and broken people let the giftedness of the kingdom shape their attitude to others.

In what ways are you feeling your brokenness today? Pause to bring it to Jesus, and rest in the promise of his words here.

4. This is not what we usually think of as leading to happiness! What might the devil want us to believe instead? Write your own list of "the devil's Beatitudes" by writing alternative slogans about how to live well that turn each of Jesus' declarations on its head.
   - Verse 3
   - Verse 4
   - Verse 5
   - Verse 6
   - Verse 7

- Verse 8

- Verse 9

- Verses 10-12

Apply

5. Look over your answers for question 4. Which of those lies are you most likely to believe, and in what situation?

6. In that situation, what would it look like for you to instead live like the "blessed" person Jesus describes?

Investigate

📖 **Read Matthew 5:17-20**

DICTIONARY

The Law / Prophets (v 17): two parts of the Old Testament Jewish Scriptures.

Pharisees / teachers of the law (v 20): religious leaders who thought they could be saved through their religious effort.

7. What do these verses tell us about how Christians should think about the laws of the Old Testament?

One of the ways Jesus fulfils the law is by doing something the prophets had promised God would do: Jesus writes God's law *on our hearts* (Jeremiah 31:31-34). He's going to put his Spirit in his people so that we *want* to obey God because we *love* God (Ezekiel 36:25-27). We surpass the righteousness of the Pharisees not by making an even greater effort than they did but by admitting we're "poor in spirit" (Matthew 5:3).

In verses 21-48, Jesus makes this new life very practical. For each topic...

- Jesus presents the command of the law: the traditional version of righteousness.
- Jesus shows how this is fulfilled in the heart: how the law is written on the heart.
- Jesus presents a practical step: a way to take the initiative to break the cycles of escalating sin.

Read Matthew 5:21-48

8. Fill in the table over the page. Under "practical step", identify both what Jesus says in this passage and what an equivalent fulfilment of the heart command might look like in your modern-day setting.

Topic	Traditional Command	Heart Fulfilment	Practical Step
Violence (v 21-26)			
Lust (v 27-32)			
Suspicion and dishonesty (v 33-37)			
Revenge (v 38-48)			

Explore More | OPTIONAL

In chapter 6, Jesus warns against hypocrisy: doing the right thing for the wrong reason. "Be careful not to practise your righteousness in front of others to be seen by them. If you do, you will have no reward from your Father in heaven" (Matthew 6:1).

- In each of following instances, what does the hypocrite do, and why? What is the result? What alternative does Jesus call for from his disciples?
  - 6:2-4
  - 6:5-6
  - 6:16-18
  - 7:1-5

Getting Personal | OPTIONAL

"Enter through the narrow gate. For wide is the gate and broad is the road that leads to destruction, and many enter through it. But small is the gate and narrow the road that leads to life, and only a few find it." (Matthew 7:13-14)

Jesus ends the Sermon on the Mount with a series of choices we must make as we respond (7:13-27). We might suppose the choice is between a good life and a bad life. But when you look back over the Sermon, that's not what you see. The options Jesus presents are between self-reliance and reliance on God; between a good life lived for the wrong reasons and a good life that arises from God's grace.

Which choice are you making before God today?

Apply

9. Think over your Christian life. What evidence do you see of the law being written on your heart? How has the Spirit changed your desires and caused you to want to obey God because you love him?

10. How have you seen people in your church community living out the ethics and attitudes of the Sermon on the Mount in the way they treat one another?

11. What practical steps do you need to take to break the cycle of escalating sin?

Pray

"Ask and it will be given to you; seek and you will find; knock and the door will be opened to you. For everyone who asks receives; the one who seeks finds; and to the one who knocks, the door will be opened.

"Which of you, if your son asks for bread, will give him a stone? Or if he asks for a fish, will give him a snake? If you, then, though you are evil, know how to give good gifts to your children, how much more will your Father in heaven give good gifts to those who ask him!" (Matthew 7:7-11)

Praise God for the evidence of his work in your heart; admit your spiritual poverty and need of him; and ask him to help you change in the ways in which this study has highlighted. Pray for a wholehearted desire to please him.

Finish your time by together praying the words that Jesus taught his disciples, in Matthew 6:9-13.

4

The King's Authority

Matthew 8:23 - 9:8; 10:1-31

The Story So Far...

Through Jesus' genealogy and the story of his birth, Matthew has introduced him as God's promised King—come to save people of all nations from their sin.

Jesus was baptised by John to show his identification with sinful humanity; then he resisted Satan's temptations in the wilderness, passing the test on our behalf.

In the Sermon on the Mount, Jesus offered his Kingdom to those who admit their brokenness. He changes our hearts so we can live his way.

Talkabout

1. What's your idea of a perfect world? If you were redesigning the world from scratch, what would you change?

Investigate

Matthew closes off the previous section of teaching in his usual way: "When Jesus had finished saying these things…" (7:28). It's an echo of Genesis 2:2: "By the seventh day God had finished the work he had been doing". God created the world through his word. Now Jesus is re-creating the world through his words. It's a world of cleansing, welcome, healing, freedom, calm and life—one in which the threats of illness, evil, natural disaster and even death meet their match in the authority of God's Saviour-King.

Matthew gives us a glimpse of this world in chapters 8 – 9. There are ten miracle stories in these chapters—nine stories in three groups (8:1-17; 8:23 – 9:8; 9:18-34), with one story containing two miracles (9:18-26). In this session we'll look at the second of those three groups.

Read Matthew 8:23 – 9:8

DICTIONARY

Blaspheming (9:3): disrespecting or mocking God, or in some way putting yourself in God's place.

2. What does Jesus demonstrate his authority over in 8:23-27, and how?

    - How do people respond to his authority?

3. What does Jesus demonstrate his authority over in verses 28-34, and how?

    - How do people respond to his authority?

4. What does Jesus demonstrate his authority over in 9:1-8, and how?

- How do people respond to his authority?

Apply

5. What do these three stories tell us about the re-created world that Jesus is bringing about? Why is that good news for you this week?

6. Look back at the different responses to Jesus' authority in these three stories. Have you observed people responding in similar ways to Jesus' authoritative claims when they encounter the gospel message? How?

7. Which of the responses in this passage do you think we should be seeking to mirror? What would that look like for you tomorrow?

Explore More | OPTIONAL

In Matthew 9:9-13 the human author of the Gospel enters the story.

📖 **Read Matthew 9:9-13**

- What does this incident teach us about Jesus' mission? Why is this good news for us?

Matthew is a tax collector, which means he's a collaborator with the occupying Roman army—a traitor to the nation and an enemy of God. So his inclusion in Jesus' kingdom is like a litmus test of the Pharisees' hearts. They performed their religious duties (offering sacrifices), but the love they professed was empty. What God really wants are people who show mercy to others because they've received mercy from God (v 13).

- Who might be the equivalent of "tax collectors" in your world? Would you be delighted to see them receive God's blessing of salvation? Or would you be shocked that they should so easily be forgiven?
- Matthew tells his story and opens his home to share Jesus with others. How could you do that this month?

Getting Personal | OPTIONAL

Pause to scan your eyes over the rest of Matthew 8 – 9. Notice who's welcoming the coming of the kingdom of Jesus. A Roman centurion and his servant; a fisherman's mother-in-law; two demon-possessed men from an area with unclean pigs; a tax-collector and his friends; an unclean woman; a dead girl; the blind and the mute. This bore no relation to the guest list of the religious leaders! Outsiders and outcasts, enemies and strangers, notorious sinners, the troubled and broken, the sick and unclean. This is divine grace in action. Who's on your guest list?

Investigate

Matthew 9 ends with Jesus looking on the crowds with compassion and inviting his disciples to pray for more workers (9:36-38). In chapter 10 he commissions the Twelve to be those workers. Their first assignment is a short-term mission trip...

Read Matthew 10:1-31

DICTIONARY

Gentiles / Samaritans (v 5): non-Jews.
Sodom and Gomorrah (v 15): two towns destroyed as judgment on their sin in Genesis 19.
Son of Man (v 23): an all-powerful human ruler (see Daniel 7:13-14) i.e. Jesus.
Beelzebul (v 25): the devil.

8. Where does Jesus tell the Twelve to go (v 5-6)?

- What are they told to do (v 7-8), and how are they going to do it (v 1)?

9. Why might the disciples have cause to be afraid at this assignment (v 14-25)?

10. Why don't they need to be afraid, according to Jesus?
    - Verses 18-20

    - Verses 26-27

    - Verses 28-31

Apply

On the day of Pentecost, mission moved into a different mode. Now the church reaches out to Gentiles (as well as Jews), and missionaries are in it for the long haul. But like the Twelve, we can still expect the Holy Spirit to speak through us (v 20): "We are therefore Christ's ambassadors, as though God were making his appeal through us" (2 Corinthians 5:20).

11. What are your fears when it comes to evangelism?

12. How does what we've read speak into those fears?

Getting Personal | OPTIONAL

Who is the person in your life that you are most fearful about sharing Jesus with?

If you're facing hostility for your faith, this is Christ's promise: *You will not fall to the ground outside your Father's care* (Matthew 10:29). The hostility may not go away, and it could even end in death. But God is in every detail (v 30), you are a precious to him (v 31), and he will bring you safely home to glory.

Pray

Praise Jesus that he is the King, re-creating our broken world, and pray that you would respond to his authority with joyful worship and courageous witness.

You could spend time praying for mission partners that you support as a church as well as for individuals you are seeking to share the good news with.

5

The Kingdom Resisted

Matthew 12:1-14; 13:24-46

The Story So Far...

Jesus was baptised by John to show his identification with sinful humanity; then he resisted Satan's temptations in the wilderness, passing the test on our behalf.

In the Sermon on the Mount, Jesus offered his kingdom to those who admit their brokenness. He changes our hearts so we can live his way.

Jesus' miracles demonstrated his authority over evil, sin, sickness and the natural world. He sent out his disciples with authority to proclaim the kingdom.

Talkabout

1. Describe your typical Sunday.

Investigate

We've seen the authority of Jesus in Matthew 8 – 9. We've seen that authority passed on to his disciples in chapter 10. Now we begin to see the authority of Jesus being resisted, just as chapter 10 anticipated.

Matthew 11:1 signals the end a section of teaching and the start of a new section of stories: "After Jesus had finished instructing his twelve disciples..." We'll pick it up in chapter 12.

Read Matthew 12:1-14

DICTIONARY

Sabbath (v 1): Saturday, the Jewish holy day. Under God's Old Testament law, people had to rest from all work on the Sabbath.

Consecrated bread (v 4): the bread of the Presence in the tabernacle/temple (see note below).

2. How do we see the Pharisees' opposition to Jesus escalate over the course of this episode?
   - Verse 2
   - Verse 10
   - Verse 14

In the Old Testament, the bread of the Presence was placed in the tabernacle as a picture of God's invitation to fellowship. When David was on the run, he entered the tabernacle (which only priests could do) and took this bread, which had been consecrated for God's use (1 Samuel 21:1-6). Yet the Scriptures do not condemn him for this. Jesus also reminds the Pharisees that the priests break the law by "working" on the Sabbath as they serve in the temple. In both cases, someone breaks the letter of the law to keep the spirit of the law.

3. What do we learn here about what God intended the Sabbath for?
   - Matthew 12:7

   - Verses 11-13

4. Why does Jesus have the right to say what the law truly means (v 6, 8)?

Getting Personal | OPTIONAL

Right before this incident, we hear these words from Jesus:

"Come to me, all you who are weary and burdened, and I will give you rest. Take my yoke upon you and learn from me, for I am gentle and humble in heart, and you will find rest for your souls. For my yoke is easy and my burden is light." (Matthew 11:28-30)

Service becomes a burden if we do it in our own strength, or if we serve Jesus to prove ourselves. We need to "learn from" Jesus that we don't need to work hard to win God's approval because we already have it in Christ, and we don't need to overwork to secure our future because our lives are safe in God's care.

Are you at risk of becoming weary in your service of Jesus? How do these words help you to rest in him?

Apply

Christians may not be bound by the Sabbath in the same way as the Israelites; but we're still called to pursue a weekly rhythm of a day of rest and worship.

5. Does the way you use your Sunday bring rest, or is it a burden? What could you do differently?

6. How could you use your Sunday to bring rest to, or relieve the burdens of, someone in your church family?

Investigate

It's been a day of disputes in Matthew 12. Is Jesus God's King establishing God's kingdom? If so, where's the defeat of God's enemies? In chapter 13, Jesus responds to these questions "that same day" (v 1) by telling a series of parables about the kingdom of heaven.

Why parables? Jesus tells his disciples it's "because the knowledge of the secrets of the kingdom of heaven has been given to you, but not to them" (v 11). These "secrets" are not that the kingdom itself is coming—every faithful Jew expected that. Instead, the secret of the kingdom is that *the kingdom comes secretly*. While the kingdom will come in glory in the future (there will be a day of judgment), it's already come in a secret, hidden, gracious way (in Jesus' offer of forgiveness).

All the parables in Matthew 13 reinforce these secrets of the kingdom. Jesus is making two points:

- The kingdom *is coming* in grace, even though it hasn't yet come in power.
- The kingdom *will come* in power, even though it's already come in grace.

Read Matthew 13:24-46

7. Look at the parables of the mustard seed and the yeast (v 31-33). How do they reveal the two secrets of the kingdom?
    - The kingdom is coming in grace.

- The kingdom will come in power.

8. Look at the parable of the weeds (v 24-30, 36-43). How does it reveal the two secrets of the kingdom?
    - The kingdom is coming in grace.

    - The kingdom will come in power.

Getting Personal | OPTIONAL

The people of Israel in Jesus' day were hoping that God would come in judgment against his enemies. But the fact is that we're all God's enemies. Jesus could have come in power, but that would have meant judgment for his people. So first Jesus came to be judged in our place. He came in grace. This was the way—the only way—that the restoration of God's kingdom can be good news for rebels like us.

Pause for a moment of quiet to express your gratitude to him.

9. Look at the parables of the treasure and the pearl (v 44-46). How do these prompt us to respond to the secrets of the kingdom, and why?

Explore More | OPTIONAL

Read Matthew 13:1-23

- How does the parable of the sower reveal the two secrets of the kingdom?
- What does this parable suggest we should expect to happen as people hear the message of the kingdom?
- How does this parable encourage us as we seek to share the message of the kingdom?

Apply

10. Based on these parables, what would you say to…
    - an older person in your church family who says, "Things were so much better when I was young. The church had real influence in our culture back then. Now things are going downhill."
    - a younger person in your church family who says, "My friends think Christianity is an absolute joke. I'm not sure following Jesus is worth the grief I get. They seem to get on fine without him."

Pray

Thank God for the ways you see his kingdom coming in grace.

Praise God that one day it will come in power.

Ask for his help to persevere in faith, labour in his strength, and rest in all that Jesus has done for you.

6

Peter's Hits and Misses

Matthew 14:22-36; 16:13-28

The Story So Far...

In the Sermon on the Mount, Jesus offered his kingdom to those who admit their brokenness. He changes our hearts so we can live his way.

Jesus' miracles demonstrated his authority over evil, sin, sickness and the natural world. He sent out his disciples with authority to proclaim the kingdom.

When opposition from the Pharisees escalated, Jesus taught through parables that his kingdom is both coming now in grace and will one day come in power.

Talkabout

1. Imagine a non-Christian friend asks you, "So, who exactly was this Jesus you Christians go on about?" How would you answer?

"Who is Jesus?" and "How will you respond to him?" are the key questions swirling around in this next section of Matthew's Gospel.

Investigate

Read Matthew 14:22-36

2. We've already seen the disciples in a boat in rough weather (8:23-27). What is similar about this encounter? What's different this time?

3. This passage is rich with allusions to the Old Testament. Read Job 9:8, Isaiah 43:1-2 and Exodus 3:13-14. In light of these passages, what is Matthew telling us about who Jesus is, do you think? (Note that when Jesus says, "It is I" in verse 27, it is literally "I am".)

4. Matthew is the only Gospel to include the story of Peter walking on the water. What do you think Matthew wants us to learn from it?

Getting Personal | OPTIONAL

This isn't the only place in Matthew's Gospel where Peter's faith falters. After Jesus is arrested, he'll fall again by denying that he even knows him (26:69-75)—but that too is a fall from which Jesus will ultimately lift him.

How shaky does your faith feel right now? Take heart. Our faith may fail as Peter's does, but Jesus remains faithful. Jesus will catch hold of us when we fall (14:31).

Explore More | OPTIONAL

In 14:31 Peter has "little faith". But in Matthew 15 we meet a woman who has "great faith".

Read Matthew 15:21-28

- Where is this woman from (v 21-22), and why is that significant?
- Given that, what is surprising about who she says Jesus is (v 22)?
- Jesus says that she has "great faith" (v 28). How do we see that in her conversation with Jesus (v 22-27)? Why do you think Jesus rebuffs her three times?

Apply

5. What is the "wind" that you're tempted to look at and become fearful of? What gives you that sinking feeling?

6. How can we help one another to fix our eyes on Jesus when walking through the storms of life? Be specific. (Perhaps try helping one another to look to Jesus in your fears right now!)

Investigate

In chapter 14 we saw Peter wavering between belief and unbelief. But as we reach a central moment in Matthew's story, Peter gains clarity.

Read Matthew 16:13-20

DICTIONARY

Elijah, Jeremiah (v 14): two of God's prophets in the Old Testament.

Hades (v 18): the realm of the dead.

7. What does Peter now believe about who Jesus is (v 16)?

It's quite a contrast! As recently as verses 8-9, the disciples were still not getting it ("You of little faith ... Do you still not understand?"). And the people referred to in verse 14 are equally confused about who Jesus is.

8. So why does Peter "get it" now, according to Jesus (v 17)?

Jesus orders his disciples not to tell anyone he's the Messiah (v 20) because they don't yet understand what it means for him to be the Messiah. That's what he's about to teach them...

Read Matthew 16:21-28

9. What has Peter misunderstood about what it means for Jesus to be the Messiah?

10. What does Jesus say about what it means for us to be his disciples?

- It's a big demand. Is it worth it?

Apply

11. In question 1 we imagined a non-Christian friend asking, "So, who exactly was this Jesus you Christians go on about?" How would you answer now, in light of this study? Take the truths we've considered and see if you can express them in a way that someone completely unfamiliar with Christianity would understand.

- How would you explain to them what it means to be a Christian, based on the truths we've considered in these verses?

Getting Personal | OPTIONAL

Which non-Christian friend would you most like to see who Jesus really is? Will you pray for an opportunity to share what we've spoken about with them soon? And will you pray for your Father in heaven to reveal the truth to them, as he did to Peter?

Pray

Thank Jesus that he is with you through the storms of life—ask for his help to keep your eyes fixed on him in faith.

Praise Jesus that he was willing to suffer and die for us as our Messiah—ask for his help to follow him on the path of self-denial.

7

The First, Last and the Last, First

Matthew 20:1-16; 21:1-32

The Story So Far...

Jesus' miracles demonstrated his authority over evil, sin, sickness and the natural world. He sent out his disciples with authority to proclaim the kingdom.

When opposition from the Pharisees escalated, Jesus taught through parables that his kingdom is both coming now in grace and will one day come in power.

Jesus revealed that he is the Messiah, who must die for his friends. Jesus called his disciples to likewise deny themselves, take up their cross and follow him.

Talkabout

1. Think of some examples of the last coming first or the first coming last—great sporting comebacks or failures, unlikely victories or defeats from history, or unexpected reversals of fortune from books or films.

Investigate

The start of Matthew 19 marks another new section in Matthew's Gospel, with Jesus leaving Galilee and stepping closer to his death in

Jerusalem (v 1). As the chapter unfolds, Jesus meets some little children with nothing to offer, who are welcomed by him (v 13-15), and a rich (but self-righteous) man who walks away sad (v 16-22).

Jesus tells his astonished disciples, "Many who are first will be last, and many who are last will be first" (v 30). That theme continues in another parable.

Read Matthew 20:1-16

DICTIONARY

Denarius (v 2, 9, 10): a coin that was the normal daily wage for a labourer.

2. Retell the parable in your own words.

3. Who are "the first" in this parable, and what do they end up with? Who are "the last", and what do they end up with?

- Are the workers who were hired early hard done by? Why, or why not?

4. What do you think this story is telling us about the kingdom of Jesus?

Getting Personal | OPTIONAL

When it comes to receiving blessing from God, we shouldn't be surprised if those blessings don't correlate with the merit of the recipient. God's generous grace doesn't work like that. That's just as well, for if we received what we deserved, we'd all be in deep trouble. But God, in his love, blesses us far above and beyond our merits.

In what ways are you experiencing God's undeserved generosity at this point in your life?

Apply

5. When might we be tempted to begrudge God's generosity to others?

6. What might that reveal about our view of the following? What would the right view be instead?
   - Ourselves
   - God
   - The kingdom

Investigate

The upside-down nature of God's kingdom and its king continues to be revealed as Jesus takes another step closer to Jerusalem.

Read Matthew 21:1-19

DICTIONARY

Daughter Zion (v 5): another name for Jerusalem.

Son of David (v 9): the promised king in King David's line.

7. What is surprising about Jesus' choice of transportation?

- What is significant about it? What does it reveal about who he is and what he's come to do?

8. Who does Jesus expel *out* of the temple, and why? Who does he welcome *in*?

Explore More | OPTIONAL

Read Malachi 3:1-2

- Where have we seen a messenger preparing the way in Matthew?
- What does Malachi say will happen next, after the messenger?
- How does this prophecy shed light on what is going on in these verses in Matthew 21?

9. The incident with the fig tree is an enacted parable about the temple (v 18-19). What is the message, do you think?

Later, Jesus makes things even clearer with a series of parables directed at the religious leaders.

Read Matthew 21:28-32

10. Who do the two sons in the story represent?

- If the religious leaders want to be "first" in the kingdom of God, what do they need to do?

Apply

11. What warnings might there be for us in this section of Matthew?

- What is the good news that we can take comfort in?

12. If we truly believe that "the last will be first, and the first will be last" in Jesus' kingdom, how might that shape how we do things in church life?

Getting Personal | OPTIONAL

How will you show Jesus' heart for the last at church this Sunday?

Pray

"'My house will be called
a house of prayer for all nations.'
The Sovereign LORD declares—
he who gathers the exiles of Israel:
'I will gather still others to them
besides those already gathered.'" (Isaiah 56:7-8)

Today, God's temple is his church. So let's be a house of prayer!

Thank God that you are among those he has gathered into his people—entirely by his grace alone. Pray that God would guard you from self-righteousness, grow you in humility, and that together you would increasingly reflect the truth that in Jesus' kingdom, "the last will be first, and the first will be last".

8

The Death of the King

Matthew 26:31-56; 27:32-54

The Story So Far...

When opposition from the Pharisees escalated, Jesus taught through parables that his kingdom is both coming now in grace and will one day come in power.

Jesus revealed that he is the Messiah, who must die for his friends. Jesus called his disciples to likewise deny themselves, take up their cross and follow him.

Jesus taught that "the last will be first, and the first will be last". He enacted judgment on the rotten temple system but offers to peace to the repentant.

Talkabout

1. Share about a time when you wanted to keep your word to someone but did not. What got in your way?

Investigate

Matthew's Gospel is now moving towards its climax—but it's all on Jesus' timeline, as Jesus again predicts his death in 26:1-2. The chief priests and elders will scheme against him, and Judas will betray him, but Jesus is the one who presses "go". The passion of Christ will unfold according to God's plan revealed in the Scriptures.

That continues to be made clear as, following their celebration of the Passover, Jesus and his disciples make their way to the Mount of Olives.

Read Matthew 26:31-46

DICTIONARY

This cup (v 39, 42): a picture of God's wrath against sin from the Old Testament (e.g. in Jeremiah 25:15).

Spirit (v 41): here, Peter's will/determination.

2. How do the disciples rate their determination and faithfulness to Jesus (v 31-35)? What does Jesus think?

3. Verses 36-46 present the disciples with an opportunity to prove their mettle! How do they fare?

4. Jesus is also being tested here. What is the temptation that he faces? How does he fare?

- How do these verses underline the intensity of this moment for Jesus?

- What would the consequences be for us if Jesus had said yes to this temptation in the garden?

Read Matthew 26:47-56

DICTIONARY

Rabbi (v 49): teacher.

Legions (v 53): military units of as many as 6,000 soldiers.

5. How does Jesus show his control of the situation in these verses?

- Why is he willing to embrace death in this way?

Explore More | OPTIONAL

Peter is tested again before the night is over. How will he fare this time?

Read Matthew 26:69-75

- How does Peter compare in this scene to the one in verses 31-35?
- What is significant about the number of times that Peter disowns Jesus? (Look back at verses 36-44.)

Read Matthew 27:11-14

- Compare these verses with Isaiah 53:7. What hope is there for weak and faithless Peter in this moment?
- Imagine the early readers of Matthew's Gospel. They would have known Peter "the Rock" as a founding apostle of the church. What impact might reading this story of his failure have had on them, do you think?

Apply

Jesus says to Peter, "The spirit is willing, but the flesh is weak" (Matthew 26:41). We know Peter's spirit is willing because he's just declared undying loyalty (v 35). But Peter hasn't come to terms with his weakness.

It's easy to see a similar pattern in our own lives—passionately declaring our love for Jesus one moment, and withering under pressure or temptation the next.

6. What should we do in light of our weakness, according to Jesus (v 41)? What does that mean, do you think?

 - Are there specific ways you could build "watch and pray" into your life this week?

 - How can we help one another?

Getting Personal | OPTIONAL

Jesus is our model because, when he faced temptation, he turned to God in prayer. But the good news of the gospel is not that we have a model—it's that we have a Saviour! Jesus covers our past because we're forgiven in him, and Jesus secures our future because we're righteous in him. The cup of God's wrath that should have been ours has already been drained by Christ. He was faithful to God in the power of the Spirit, and now his faithful record is ours.

Pause to enjoy that truth and thank Jesus for it.

Investigate

After his arrest, Jesus is tried by the Sanhedrin, questioned by the Roman governor Pilate and then sentenced to death by crucifixion.

Read Matthew 27:32-54

In verses 45-54, Matthew describes Jesus' death from three perspectives with three matching consequences.

7. What is the experience for Jesus described in verses 45-46?

- What is the consequence for us, represented in verse 51?

8. What is the experience for Jesus described in verses 47-49?

- What is the consequence for us, hinted at in verse 54?

9. What is the experience for Jesus described in verse 50?

- What is the consequence for us, previewed in verses 52-53?

Getting Personal | OPTIONAL

Look over the three perspectives on Jesus' death described in questions 7-9. Which one is particularly precious to you at the moment?

Apply

10. How does what we've read help us when…
    - we feel the weight of guilt for our sin?
    - we are suffering and feel abandoned by God?

Pray

There could be no better response to this passage than to worship the God we see revealed at the cross:

- *A God so loving that he dies for his people.*
- *A God so powerful that he is not afraid to lay aside his majesty.*
- *A God so majestic that his glory shines bright even under darkened skies.*
- *A God so wise that he conquers through apparent defeat.*
- *A God so gracious that he opens his arms to welcome his enemies.*

9

The King Lives

Matthew 28:1-10, 16-20

The Story So Far...

Jesus revealed that he is the Messiah, who must die for his friends. Jesus called his disciples to likewise deny themselves, take up their cross and follow him.

Jesus taught that "the last will be first, and the first will be last". He enacted judgment on the rotten temple system but offers to peace to the repentant.

Despite intense temptation to do otherwise, Jesus allowed himself to be arrested and killed. His death brings life, reveals God's love and unites us to him.

Talkabout

1. What have been some of the recurring themes you've noticed as we've studied Matthew's Gospel?

Matthew is about to take many of those themes and hold them up to us in stunning new ways in this glorious conclusion to his Gospel.

Investigate

Matthew has described Jesus' death and burial. But that's not the end of the story.

📖 Read Matthew 28:1-10

2. Put yourself in Mary Magdalene's and the other Mary's shoes for a moment. What else have they witnessed in the past three days (see 27:55-56, 59-61)?

    - What do you think they were expecting to find on that Sunday morning? What did they see instead?

3. Why might it be significant that it's two women who play a key part in the action on this momentous morning?

4. Matthew doesn't usually give precise indicators of time in his Gospel, but he begins his resurrection account with two (28:1). What might they tell us about what the resurrection represents? (Hint: Part of it has something to do with the creation account in Genesis 1!)

5. The women have two encounters: one with an angel and one with Jesus. What are they told in both cases (v 5, 10)? Why might that reassurance have been necessary?!

Apply

This is the message of the resurrection: Jesus has risen to end our fear.

6. Why does the resurrection mean we don't need to fear sin?

- Why does the resurrection mean we don't need to fear people?

Getting Personal | OPTIONAL

In what ways or in what circumstances do you experience either of these two fears? What might the risen Lord Jesus say to you, in the face of that fear?

Explore More | OPTIONAL

Matthew's account of the resurrection is not that long, yet he spends almost two-fifths of it proving the reality of the resurrection. Let's take a look at his evidence.

Read Matthew 27:57-66; 28:11-15

- What details does Matthew provide us with to counter the claims that...
    - Jesus merely fainted on the cross and revived in the tomb?
    - Jesus' body was stolen—the resurrection was a hoax?
- Why is it important that what happened on the first Easter Sunday was a real resurrection?
- What possibility do the chief priests fail to consider in 28:12? What does that tell us about the nature of their unbelief, do you think?

Investigate

Unlike the other Gospel writers, Matthew doesn't tell us about Jesus' resurrection appearances in Jerusalem. Instead, in 28:7 and 10, the women are instructed to tell the disciples to meet Jesus in Galilee (just as he had said in 26:32). All the action points there.

Back in 4:12-17, Jesus "withdrew to Galilee" to fulfil Isaiah's prophecy of light dawning in "Galilee of the Gentiles" (Isaiah 9:1-7). The miracles and preaching of Jesus were the first ray of light on the horizon. Now the light of God's salvation is about to radiate out from Galilee to all nations.

Read Matthew 28:16-20

7. Jesus says that "all authority" has been given to him (v 18). How have we seen him display his complete authority already in Matthew's Gospel?

   - What has changed (and what is about to change) at this point? (See 26:64 and Acts 1:9-11.)

   - What appropriate response to Jesus' authority do we see in Matthew 28:17 (and also verse 9)?

Getting Personal | OPTIONAL

Matthew leaves us with two options: worship or doubt. Verse 17 says, "When they saw him, they worshipped him; but some doubted". Matthew is asking us to place ourselves in one of these two camps: will we worship Jesus, or will we doubt him? There's no neutrality. If Christ is risen, then Christ must be worshipped, with our lips and lives.

8. What connection is there between Jesus' command in verse 19 and his statement in verse 18?

9. Why is this a fitting end to Matthew's Gospel, given what we've read so far?

10. It's a big mission! What reassurance does Jesus give his disciples?

Apply

Do you feel the logic of the resurrection?

- Jesus has risen, and therefore he is Lord.
- Jesus is Lord, and therefore he claims the nations.
- Jesus claims the nations, and therefore he sends us to call people to repentance.

11. Global mission is not a niche interest for Christians. We're all called to play our part. What does that already look like for you (as an individual and as part of your church)? How would you like it to look in the future?

12. How do Jesus' words in verses 18-19 challenge you?

- How do they bring you comfort?

- How do they inspire your courage?

Pray

Worship the risen Lord Jesus: the one with all authority, with us by his Spirit.

Pray for mission partners known to you, engaged in the work of the Great Commission.

Pray for friends and family closer to home with whom you would like to share the gospel.

Matthew

Kingdom Treasure

LEADER'S GUIDE

Leader's Guide: Introduction

This Leader's Guide includes guidance for every question. It will provide background information and help you if you get stuck. For each session, you'll also find the following:

The Big Idea: The main point of the session, in brief. This is what you should be aiming to have fixed in people's minds by the end of the session!

Summary: An overview of the passage you're reading together.

Optional Extra: Usually this is an introductory activity that ties in with the main theme of the Bible study and is designed to break the ice at the beginning of a session. Or it may be a "homework project" that people can tackle during the week.

Occasionally the Leader's Guide includes an extra follow-up question, printed in ***italics***. This doesn't appear in the main study guide but could be a useful add-on to help your group get to the answer or go deeper.

Here are a few key principles to bear in mind as you prepare to lead:

- Don't just read out the answers from the Leader's Guide. Ideally, you want the group to discover these answers from the Bible for themselves.
- Keep drawing people back to the passage you're studying. People may come up with answers based on their experiences or on teaching they've heard in the past, but the point of this study is to listen to God's word itself—so keep directing your group to look at the text.
- Make sure everyone finishes the session knowing how the passage is relevant for them. We do Bible study so that our lives can be changed by what we hear from God's word. So, **Apply** questions aren't just an add-on—they're a vital part of the session.

Finally, remember that your group is unique! You should feel free to use this Good Book Guide in a way that works for them. If they're a quiet bunch, you might want to spend longer on the **Talkabout** question. If they love to get creative, try using mind-mapping or doodling to kick-start some of your discussions. If your time is limited, you can choose to skip **Explore More** or split the whole session into two. Adapt the material in whatever way you think will help your group get the most out of God's word.

1

The Promised One

Matthew 1:1 - 2:12

The Big Idea

Jesus is God's promised King—God himself come to save people of all nations from their sin. The proper response is worship.

Summary

Matthew packs his account of the Nativity with references to the Old Testament, beginning with a genealogy (1:1). For Matthew's Jewish readers, it would have evoked a succession of stories, all of which are about to converge on Mary's child.

Matthew orders this list in a particular way (leaving a few people out in the process to make the numbers work): "Thus there were fourteen generations in all from Abraham to David, fourteen from David to the exile to Babylon, and fourteen from the exile to the Messiah" (v 17). The groups of fourteen focus on three key moments and what they show us about who Jesus is:

- Abraham: the father of the Jewish nation (v 2). Jesus is the true son of Abraham: the one who reverses the curse, bringing blessing to all nations.
- David: Israel's greatest king (v 6). Israelite kings were anointed with oil, so the promised King was known as "the anointed one". The Greek word for this is "Christ", and the Hebrew word is "Messiah" (v 1, 16). Jesus is God's promised King, coming to set not only Israel but humanity free.
- Babylon: the time when the Jews went into exile (v 12). Although in time Ezra and Nehemiah led the people back to the land, they still weren't free (Nehemiah 9:36-37). The underlying issues of human sin and divine judgment had not been addressed. Jesus is the one who will lead us home. He not only shows us the way back to God; he himself is "the way" (John 14:6).

The second half of the session briefly takes in Matthew 1:18-25—noting how Matthew spotlights Jesus as God himself coming to save his people from sin—before looking at the responses to Jesus on display in 2:1-12. Herod and the Jewish leaders are threatened by this new king and will seek to eliminate him. In contrast, the pagan Magi rightly worship him (v 2, 11). This is an early sign of Matthew's concern for global mission and the inclusion of Gentiles in the people of God (a theme to which we will return in Matthew 28). Today, though, the challenge to us is this: are we going to follow the example of Herod, seeing Jesus as a rival to eradicate from our lives? Or are we going to follow the example of the Magi, seeing Jesus as Immanuel and worshipping him with our lives?

Optional Extra

To introduce Matthew's genealogy and recap Old Testament history, write the following names/event on separate pieces of paper, and ask the group to work together to put them in the right order (they can do this while looking at Matthew 1:1-17 if you think they'll need some help): Abraham, Isaac, Jacob, Judah, Boaz and Ruth, David, Solomon, Hezekiah; the Exile; Joseph and Mary; Jesus the Messiah.

Guidance for Questions

1. **Imagine you were going to introduce another member of your group to someone they didn't know (at a party or after church, or similar). What would you say about them by way of introduction?**
   Perhaps we'd say something about what they do or where they're from or how we know them. It would probably depend on who we were introducing them to—we'd look for shared interests or highlight points of connection. Matthew introduces us to Jesus with a genealogy (1:1). This list of names is like the contents page of the Old Testament. For Matthew's Jewish readers, it would have evoked a succession of stories, all of which are about to converge on Mary's child.

2. **Matthew orders his genealogy to focus on three moments in particular from Israel's history. What are they (v 17)?**
   - Abraham: the father of the nation (v 2).
   - David: Israel's greatest king (v 6).
   - Babylon: the time when the Jews went into exile (v 12).

   If some members of your group are likely to be largely unfamiliar with the Old Testament, take time to gauge how much they know about these figures and fill in the headlines, before moving on to questions 3 – 5.

3. **Read Genesis 12:1-3. What does the connection with Abraham in Matthew 1 show us about what Jesus is going to do?**
   In Genesis 12 God promised that through Abraham's offspring, the curse would be reversed. Our relationship with God would be restored, human relationships would be mended, and the earth would be made new. The message of Matthew's genealogy is that this promise has passed down the generations until we meet Mary and her child. Jesus is the true son of Abraham: the one who reverses the curse of Genesis 3, bringing blessing to all nations.

- ***OPTIONAL: Read Galatians 3:13-14. How was Jesus going to bring this blessing?***
  By bearing the curse for us.

4. **Read God's words to King David in 2 Samuel 7:11b-16. What does the connection with King David in Matthew 1 show us about what Jesus is going to do?**
   The curse came because humanity rebelled against God's rule. God's rule was one of peace, provision

and protection. But Satan portrayed God as a tyrant, and humanity believed that lie. Yet, instead of finding freedom, they became enslaved to sin and self. God had every reason to write us off. But instead he made a promise to David, Israel's greatest king, that one of his descendants would set God's people free—free to enjoy life under God's rule (2 Samuel 7:10-16).

The message of Matthew's genealogy is that this promised descendant of David is Mary's child. Israelite kings were anointed with oil, so the promised king was known as "the anointed one". The Hebrew word is "Messiah" (Matthew 1:1, 16). Jesus is God's promised King, coming to set us free.

- **Why might this have looked unlikely to readers in Matthew's day, living under the Roman Empire?**
  Instead of restoring God's reign, successive Israelite kings had led people further from God. So the Davidic dynasty no longer reigned over Israel, which instead suffered under Roman occupation. But the prophets had promised a new King David, who would restore God's life-giving rule.

5. **In what way is the Exile from Babylon a picture of all of humanity's plight?**
   We're all exiles from Eden, and we're all estranged from God. That's why we're so restless. Our hearts are hard-wired for God, and yet it's as if we'll head in any direction except back to God, looking for fulfilment in our careers, homes, families, or entertainment.

- **What does this connection with the Exile to Babylon tell us about what Jesus is going to do?**
  The message of Matthew's genealogy is that the end of exile is lying in the manger. Jesus is the one who will lead us home. He not only shows us the way back to God; he himself is "the way" (John 14:6).

6. **What point do you think Matthew is making by the particular women he chooses to include (v 3, 5, 6)?**
   They are all Gentiles: Tamar and Rahab were Canaanites, Ruth was a Moabite and Bathsheba is called "Uriah's wife" to spotlight her connection to a Hittite (see Genesis 34; Joshua 2; Ruth 1 – 4; 2 Samuel 11). It's a picture of the way Jesus will weave all nations into the story of God's people.

   Moreover, three of these women come with question marks hanging over their morality. Tamar disguised herself as a prostitute to sleep with her father-in-law, forcing him to do right by her deceased husband (Genesis 34). Rahab was the Canaanite prostitute who hid two Israelite spies (Joshua 2). Bathsheba was involved in an act of adultery, though her culpability is unclear (2 Samuel 11). These names spotlight the fact that Jesus came to save Jews and Gentiles, men and women, sinners and sinned-against. (See Getting Personal.)

7. **What will happen in our hearts and lives if we lose sight of any one of these pictures of who Jesus is?**
   - We live in a cursed world with broken relationships. We need to trust God's promise of blessing. Otherwise we may despair and live for the fleeting treasures of this world.
   - We live in a rebellious world in which people mock God and disregard his reign. We need to trust God's promise that Christ will be triumphant and his people will be vindicated. Otherwise we may despair and start to align ourselves with the rebellious majority.
   - We live in a restless world in which people are exiled from God. We need to trust God's promise that Christ will lead us away from the slavery of sin to home in glory. Otherwise we may despair and give up the struggle against sin in our lives.

- **Which of those pictures gives you the most comfort and reassurance in this moment, and why?**
  This is an opportunity for your group to share ways in which these promises speak into their present concerns, fears and temptations.

8. **What do the two names given to Mary's child add to our understanding of who he is?**
   "Jesus" (v 21) is the Greek equivalent of "Joshua", which means "the LORD saves". This baby is going to deal with the problem of human sin and divine judgment. Second, Matthew comments, "'they will call him Immanuel' (which means 'God with us')" (v 23). God himself is coming to save his people from sin.

Explore More

- ***Read Isaiah 7:1-17. What problem did Ahaz face (v 1-2)?***
  Ahaz was the king of Judah. He was the descendant of David on the throne of David, just as God had promised. But he wasn't like his father David. He led the people into idolatry, even sacrificing his children. So the kings of Syria and the northern kingdom of Israel formed an alliance against him, and Ahaz was terrified (v 1-2). The house of David—the means through which God had promised to restore his reign—was in mortal danger.

- ***What promise did God offer him (v 7-9)? What did Ahaz need to do in response (v 4)?***
  Isaiah promised divine deliverance if Ahaz would entrust himself to God (v 3-9).

- ***What was that sign (v 14)? And what would it point to (v 16-17)?***
  "The virgin will conceive and give birth to a son, and will call him Immanuel" (v 14). The word "virgin" in Isaiah 7:14 means "a sexually inexperienced woman". It was usually used to describe a virgin, but not always. So, it could initially have described Isaiah's wife, who bears him a son in 8:1-4, but Matthew recognises that

its ultimate fulfilment is in the virgin Mary (Matthew 1:18).

The point is that God would bring the reign of David's sons to an end (as he did when Judah was exiled in Babylon) and then start afresh by raising up a new king from a virgin. In the meantime, Assyria would turn on Judah with devastating consequences (Isaiah 7:15-25). (Curds and honey were the food of poverty—a sign that Judah's economy would collapse.)

---

9. **What different responses to the news of Jesus' birth do we see in this passage? Why do people respond in those ways?**
   The news of a new king disturbs the Jerusalem elites (v 3), presumably because talk of another king is a threat to their cosy arrangement with the Roman occupiers. Herod asks the religious leaders where the promised Messiah is to be born (v 4), and they answer by quoting a prophecy from Micah 5:2, 4 (Matthew 2:5-6); but none of them bother to go there. Your group probably know that Herod's stated intentions in verses 7-8 are not what they seem; he will ultimately respond to Jesus' birth by trying to destroy him. Herod sees Jesus as a rival to be distinguished.

   The Magi, meanwhile, find Jesus and worship him (v 9-11). The Magi's knowledge has caused them to seek Jesus, but they need the Scriptures to locate him. They can see Jesus for who he really is.

   - **What is surprising about who responds in which way?**
     Those who know most about the Messiah are those who welcome him least! Whereas the Magi were pagans. They were not soaked in the Old Testament stories referred to in Matthew 1, yet they nevertheless went to great lengths and great expense to honour Jesus.

10. **How do we see God's promise to Abraham coming true in these verses?**
    Matthew presents Jesus as the fulfilment of the promise to Abraham: that Abraham's family will bless all nations (Genesis 12:3; Matthew 1:2). The gifts of the Magi echo the story of the queen of Sheba bringing gifts to King Solomon (1 Kings 10:10) and Isaiah's promise of tribute from the nations (Isaiah 60:1-10; see also Psalm 72:10-11), including "gold and frankincense" (Isaiah 60:6, ESV). The Magi are the only people in the story who are Gentiles (Matthew 2:1), yet they're the only people in the story who worship Jesus. Matthew's Gospel begins with the Magi worshipping Jesus, and it ends with the disciples worshipping Jesus (28:17) and being sent to call all the nations to worship Jesus too (v 19).

11. **There's a little bit of Herod in all of us. In what ways might people today be similarly "disturbed" by the idea of Jesus being King, and of having to submit to his rule? What about us?**

Some people in your group will probably be able to think of people they know who have refused the offer of the gospel because they don't want their lives to change. Even as Christians who know and love Jesus, there may be moments when we bridle at what Jesus is asking us to do. Be ready with your own examples if the group is slow to share.

- **What would it look like to respond like the Magi to Jesus instead?**
We will worship him with our lives, laying at his feet everything we have at our disposal. Discuss what this might look like practically.

12. **If Jesus is King of all the nations, how should that shape our prayers, our finances and our churches?**
Discuss ways in which you can be wholeheartedly praying for and giving to missions, and have this shape the priorities of your local church. As well as praying for the work of the gospel in other countries, for churches in urban areas there will probably be opportunities to welcome people from many nations into your own church. What would it take to reach the nations on our doorstep with the gospel and make them a full part of our church families?

2

The King Wins for Us

Matthew 3:1 - 4:11

The Big Idea

Jesus has come to identify with us (in baptism) and represent us, passing the test that Adam and Israel failed. We're called to repent in response to his coming.

Summary

In chapter 3, Matthew introduces a new character: John the Baptist. John declares, "Repent, for the kingdom of heaven has come near" (Matthew 3:2). God is coming in the person of his Son to liberate his people from a deeper, darker exile than the one of Isaiah's day (see v 3). And John is his herald who has run on ahead, as it were, to let the world know that God is on his way.

How do you prepare for the coming of God? John's call to his hearers—and Matthew's call to his readers—is to repent (v 2) and to express that repentance in baptism (v 5-6). God's coming will mean liberation for his people and judgment for his enemies. But we've all become enemies of God, and so we need to change sides.

Not everyone will be prepared to do that though (v 7-10). John speaks of the one who will come after him in terms of purging and winnowing (v 11-12). The coming of Jesus would divide 1st-century Judaism. The Pharisees and Sadducees in this passage represent those who reject Jesus, thereby confirming that they are deserving of judgment. One day, Jesus will return, with an axe and a winnowing fork in hand, as it were, to enact this judgment.

In verse 13, there is a strange twist in Matthew's story. Jesus comes to be baptised by John! The incongruity of this is not lost on John, who tries to dissuade Jesus (v 13-14). But Jesus says, "It is proper for us to do this to fulfil all righteousness" (v 15)—that is, to obey God's will. By being baptised, Jesus identifies with his sinful people and so accepts the role of the suffering servant to which God has called him (Isaiah 53:5, 12). Jesus fulfils righteousness by signalling his willingness to obey God's will, which for him will mean suffering for his people.

Jesus' obedience is also spotlighted in chapter 4, as he is led by the Spirit to be tested in the wilderness (Matthew 4:1-2). In doing this, Jesus is re-running the stories of Adam (who was tempted by Satan in Genesis 3) and Israel (who were tested by God in the wilderness for 40 years on their way to the promised land). Both Adam and Israel failed. Twice it seemed that God's plan for humanity had been derailed by human sin, but God was actually preparing us to see the true glory of Jesus. Jesus rewrites our story, and this time he writes a different ending. Israel failed to be a faithful "son" of God, "but pointed to the 'Son' who would never fail" (D.A. Carson, "Matthew," in *The Expositor's Bible Commentary*, Volume 8 (Zondervan, 1984), p. 112). Now his status as the loved and obedient son of God can become ours.

Optional Extra

Put out some extra special snacks at the start of your session, but tell your group that they're for the end. Will they pass the test and not eat them?!

Guidance for Questions

1. **Imagine that a very important visitor is going to visit your community next week. How would you prepare?**
   Perhaps you'd plant some flowers, add a fresh coat of paint, or do a litter pick. (You might have fun imagining what you'd need to do to your church building in preparation for a special visitor!) In Matthew 3:3, the voice in the wilderness calls for a major civil-engineering project to prepare for the coming of God—the construction of "a highway for our God" (Isaiah 40:3).

2. **What does John tell people that they need to do to prepare for the coming kingdom (v 2)?**
   Not road building—that was just an image. John's call to his hearers—and Matthew's call to his readers—is to repent (v 2).

- **What do the rest of these verses teach us about what that means or what it looks like?**
  Repentance is a 180-degree turn from going our own way to going God's way. It involves "confessing ... sins" and is expressed in baptism (v 6, 11). Then we are to "produce fruit in keeping with repentance" (v 8), living changed lives. The religious leaders assume that their ethnicity means their future is secure, but John warns that those who do not produce the good fruit that flows from true faith and repentance will be cut down.

3. **John has come to prepare the people. But what will the one who comes after him do, according to verses 11-12? What do the images John uses mean, do you think?**

- **Verse 11**
  John's baptism with water was merely an outward sign; Jesus would effect the reality to which John's baptism pointed. We often contrast the outward cleansing of John's baptism with the inner cleansing of Jesus' work; Jesus cleanses our hearts through the work of the Spirit, washing away our guilt and reorienting our desires. That's implicit here in the reference to baptism "with the Holy Spirit". But Matthew's focus is on another type of cleansing or baptism: Jesus will purge God's people with fire. Jesus will judge unfruitful people just as farmers burn unfruitful trees or chaff (v 10).
- **Verse 12**
  In Jesus' day, harvested wheat was first threshed to separate the wheat from its inedible outer case (the "chaff"). Then a winnowing fork (v 12) was used to throw the wheat and chaff into the air so the lighter chaff would blow away. John says Jesus is coming to winnow God's people, dividing them into those who reject Jesus, thereby confirming that they are deserving of judgment, and those who accept him. The same thing happens today as the gospel is proclaimed. One day Jesus will return, with axe and winnowing fork in hand, as it were, to enact this judgment.

4. **Given what we've read in chapter 3 so far, what is surprising about verse 13?**
   John has just said that Jesus is a greater person with a greater baptism. But then Jesus comes to be baptised by John! The incongruity of this is not lost on John, who tries to dissuade Jesus (v 14). Moreover, John's baptism is a sign of repentance linked to the confession of sin (v 2, 6), but Jesus doesn't need to repent, nor does he have any sins to confess.

5. **Why does Jesus insist on being baptised? What does this mean, do you think?**
   Jesus says, "It is proper for us to do this to fulfil all righteousness" (v 15). In Paul's writings, "righteousness" means the right standing with God that Jesus shares with his people. But in Matthew's Gospel, fulfilling righteousness

means obeying God's will. By being baptised, Jesus is obeying God's will. If your group struggles to answer this question, the note in the Study Guide after the "Explore More" section provides more clarity.

Explore More

- ***How are [these verses] echoed in Matthew 3:13-17? What clues do they give us as to what is going on in this surprising incident?***
- ***The suffering servant: Isaiah 53:5, 12; 42:1.***
  Isaiah promised a suffering servant who would redeem God's people by bearing their sin in their place (53:5, 12). By being baptised, Jesus identifies with his sinful people and so accepts the role of the suffering servant to which God has called him. Jesus fulfils righteousness by signalling his willingness to obey God's will, which for him will mean suffering for his people. This resolution is affirmed as Jesus rises from the water. As he does so, the Spirit descends "on him", and the voice of the Father echoes Isaiah's words in 42:1 (Matthew 3:16-17).
- ***The anointed King: Psalm 2:7; 2 Samuel 7:12-14.***
  The words of the Father at Jesus' baptism also echo 2 Samuel 7:14 and Psalm 2:7, which speak of God adopting King David's son as his son. Jesus is anointed and empowered by the Spirit to be God's King.
- ***Isaac, Abraham's son: Genesis 22:1-2.***
  Isaac was Abraham's son and the inheritor of God's promises, described by God to Abraham as the one "whom you love" (v 2). Jesus, too, is the beloved Son (Matthew 3:17). God told Abraham to sacrifice Isaac but spared him at the last moment. But Jesus will not be spared because he is the true sacrifice for sin.

6. **One day Jesus will return, axe and winnowing fork in hand, as it were, to enact this judgment. How can we prepare for this coming, according to these verses?**
   In the same way that they did in the 1st century: "confessing their sins, they were baptised" (v 6). And then we are to "produce fruit in keeping with repentance" (v 8). Give space to think about what this means.

- ***OPTIONAL: Think back to when you were baptised. In what ways have you grown since then?***
  This question is designed to encourage—if people in your group are genuine believers, they will be producing fruit in keeping with repentance. Be ready to point out ways in which you've seen people grow.

7. **The image of Jesus "winnowing" grain points to how the coming of Jesus would divide 1st-century Judaism (3:7-12). It still divides humanity today, as the gospel is proclaimed and people either reject**

or accept it. How does this picture of Jesus put steel into our life and witness as his followers?

This picture will inspire us with a sense of urgency. A day of judgment is coming; people do not have an unlimited amount of time to respond to Jesus. It also helps to strengthen us against the fear of rejection. Jesus has always been divisive. If the message of Jesus creates division, that's not necessarily a sign that things have gone wrong; that's a sign of his winnowing work.

8. **Look at the three tests that Jesus undergoes. For each one, how does Satan subtly offer Jesus an opt-out of the suffering he must undergo as the suffering servant?**

- **Test 1 (4:3-4; compare with 27:40)**

  Satan's first temptation is an invitation to Jesus to use his rights as God's Son to avoid the suffering he must undergo as the representative of God's people. It's a temptation that will be repeated at the cross when the crowd cries, "Come down from the cross, if you are the Son of God!" (27:40). In effect, Satan says, *You're the Son of God; so you don't have to suffer like this.* In one sense, that's true, but Jesus has laid down those rights to obey his Father and save his people.

  - ***OPTIONAL: How does this echo the tests faced by Israel in the wilderness and by Adam in the garden?***

    When Israel was hungry in the wilderness, the nation became a grumbling "son" who didn't trust their Father (Exodus 16:1-3; Deuteronomy 8:2-3). Jesus remains a trusting Son who's nourished by God's word (John 4:34). Adam sinned by eating because he doubted God's word; Jesus obeyed by abstaining because God's word sustained him (Matthew 4:4).

- **Test 2 (4:5-7; compare with 26:51-54)**

  Satan invites Jesus to prove his divine sonship by throwing himself off the temple with a view to God sending angels to rescue him (4:5-6). But Jesus doesn't need to prove his sonship. He's heard it declared by the Father, and he's happy to trust his Father's word (3:17). Again, this temptation will return during the passion of Jesus (26:53-54). The "angel option" is always there. But it would be opting out of the task God has given Jesus—the task of being the servant who suffers for his people. So Jesus responds with a quote from Deuteronomy 6:16: "Do not put the Lord your God to the test" (Matthew 4:7). Satan has taken a divine promise and twisted it into a divine test.

- **Test 3 (4:8-10)**

  The first two temptations were subtle. The third time round the temptation is clear: "Would Jesus be God's Messiah by following the path of suffering, even to death on a cross? Or would Jesus be Satan's Messiah by simply bowing down to him, and not having to die on a cross?" (Mark Jones, *Knowing Jesus* (Banner of

Truth, 2015), p. 112). Jesus dismisses Satan and chooses to serve God, even though that means accepting the cross (v 10-11).

9. **What would the consequences have been if Jesus had said yes to any of Satan's offers? What was at stake?**
Three times, Jesus rejects the option to take a shortcut to glory. He could have arrived at his destination without suffering, but he would have arrived without a people. Only by dying in our place could he secure our place alongside him in his glory.

10. **Imagine a Christian friend tells you that they are trying (and often failing) to resist temptation in some area (e.g. watching pornography, yelling at their kids, grumbling about others behind their back). How could you use Matthew 3 and 4 to help and encourage them?**
There are lessons for us here as we face temptation. Like Jesus, we're to see ourselves as children of God and so trust in his fatherly care. Like Jesus, we're to extinguish the flaming arrows of Satan's temptations and lies by countering them with the promises of God's word (Ephesians 6:16). But most importantly, we'd want to reassure our friend that, when confronted with their sin, they've already passed the test in Christ. They're already an obedient child of God because Jesus has obeyed on their behalf. If they are baptised into Christ, then God's verdict on Christ at his baptism becomes God's declaration to them: *You are my son, my daughter, whom I love; with you I am well pleased* (adapting Matthew 3:17).

11. **In what areas of your life do you need to hear the same help and encouragement?**
Give your group time and space to share. Be ready to go first with your answer if they are slow to open up.

3

The Renewed Life

Matthew 5:1-12, 17-48

The Big Idea

Jesus gives his kingdom not to the self-righteous but to those who feel their brokenness—and he changes the hearts of his people in ways that shape our attitudes to others so that we can live as his new community.

Summary

Christians generally ask two questions of the Sermon on the Mount.

First, is the sermon practical? Or is it designed for a future era or to make us realise our need of Christ? The answer is: yes, the sermon is practical. In one sense it does belong to a future era, but that future has broken into the present through Jesus. It's also true that unbelievers will find it impossible to obey, and so, yes, they ought then to realise their need of Jesus. But primarily this is an ethic for Christ's new community, living in the light of his coming and empowered by his Spirit.

Second, does it offer a personal or a social ethic? The answer is that the sermon is to be lived by the Christian community. So it's neither an individual ethic to be practised in isolation nor an ethic for society as a whole. The sermon is about how the church conducts itself in the old age while it witnesses to the coming of the new age.

The first half of the study considers the Beatitudes (5:1-12). These continue the theme of liberation that Matthew started in chapters 1 – 4. But Jesus is speaking of something much bigger than the political liberation of 1st-century Judea. He has come to liberate his people from sin and death, and lead us home to God. What would have shocked his hearers was who gets to be part of this coming kingdom. It's not the Sadducees or Pharisees, for "blessed are the poor in spirit" (5:3). It's not the Zealots (the violent revolutionaries of the day), for "blessed are the merciful" and "the peacemakers" (v 7, 9, 38-48). Instead, it's "the poor in spirit", or broken people, to whom the kingdom is given. This is how Jesus begins in verse 3, and it sets the tone for the whole sermon.

The second half of the study takes in 5:17-48. Just as Moses received the old covenant law on a mountain, so Jesus gives a new law in the Sermon on the Mount. (Compare 5:1-2 with Exodus 19:3, and Matthew 8:1 with Exodus 34:29.) Yet Moses was only God's spokesman, whereas Jesus speaks as the Law-giver ("But I tell you...")—the God of Sinai come down to lead his people. The Old Testament continues to be authoritative and relevant, but now it must be read in the light of the coming of Jesus. There is a note in the Study Guide after question 7 suggesting a framework for how we might do this, and then question 8 provides an opportunity to put that into practice.

In 5:21-48 Jesus describes a community in which people get angry, but they don't let things escalate. They take the initiative and seek to be reconciled (v 23-26). In this community people are prone to lust, but they prevent it escalating (v 27-32). In this community people don't have to swear they're telling the truth because they have a reputation for honesty, and they trust one another (v 34-37). In this community people get wronged, but instead of feuds escalating, people repay those wrongs with a blessing (v 39-42). They do good to people—even when those people have let them down (v 44).

Optional Extra

After question 4, show a couple of popular advertisements or commercials. Discuss what they are communicating about the secret to happiness. Are they more in line with the "devil's Beatitudes" or those of Jesus? Alternatively you could do this as part of question 1, to stimulate your discussion on the secret to happiness. What do the advertisers tell us?

Guidance for Questions

1. **What is the secret to happiness? How do you think your non-Christian friends, family or co-workers would answer that question?**
   Allow your group time to discuss. This question links to the first part of this study on the Beatitudes. In most translations these each begin with the word "Blessed", and this implies something God has done for us—whereas Jesus is actually describing how we are to live. A beatitude "is a pronouncement, based on observation, that a certain way of being in the world produces human flourishing and felicity" (Jonathan T. Pennington, *The Sermon on the Mount and Human Flourishing* (Baker, 2017), p. 42). The Greek word translated "blessed" carries the sense of "happy". The Beatitudes are descriptions of how we can live a good life under Christ's kingship—both individually and communally, and both now and more fully when Christ returns.

2. **Who is listening as Jesus delivers the "Sermon on the Mount" (v 1-2)? What might that tell us about how we should understand and apply this teaching today?**
   He's teaching his disciples—but "the crowds" are also listening in.
   While there are a number of ways of understanding the sermon (see *Matthew For You*, p. 41-43), I want to suggest that the sermon is primarily an ethic for the new people of God. It describes how human beings can flourish as they live in the world as part of Christ's kingdom, in communion with God. Alongside this, it critiques self-righteousness or superficial righteousness, in which a person's actions are merely for outward show. These purposes reflect the two audiences for the sermon: "his disciples" are told how to live as followers of Jesus while "the crowds" are challenged to repent of self-righteousness (v 1-2). But these two purposes

intersect because Jesus repeatedly says, *Don't be self-righteous like this... instead, be like this...*

3. **What do each of these descriptions have in common, would you say? (Look at the first half of each verse that begins "Blessed are...")**
   Verse 3 sets the tone for the whole list (and the whole sermon). Jesus comforts those who mourn over their sin (v 4). He bequeaths the earth not to the grasping but to "the meek" (v 5). He gives righteousness to those who long for righteousness (v 6). He reveals himself not to the outwardly religious but to "the pure in heart" (v 8). In summary, Jesus gives his kingdom to people who feel their brokenness. Broken people receive his kingdom as a gift, and broken people let the giftedness of the kingdom shape their attitude to others.

- **Compare verses 3 and 10 with verses 4-9. What difference do you notice?**
  The blessings of verses 3 and 10 are in the present while verses 4-9 describe what will happen in the future. The kingdom is both present and future. So Christ's liberation is already beginning among his people. Already the future kingdom is taking shape. The sermon therefore describes life under Christ's kingship—the good life we're called to embrace.

4. **This is not what we usually think of as leading to happiness! What might the devil want us to believe instead? Write your own list of the "devil's Beatitudes" by writing alternative slogans about how to live well that turn each of Jesus' declarations on its head.**
   Examples are given below, but there's no one right answer, and there's scope to be creative! You could split your group into pairs for this exercise and compare what different groups come up with.

- **Verse 3**
  Believe in yourself because you're great as you are!
- **Verse 4**
  Don't take life too seriously and shrug it off when you make mistakes.
- **Verse 5**
  Always look after No. 1 and don't let anyone put you down.
- **Verse 6**
  Avoid campaigns and causes—they're not worth the effort.
- **Verse 7**
  Demand your rights because you're worth it!
- **Verse 8**
  You'll be okay as long as you tick the right boxes.
- **Verse 9**
  Don't get involved in other people's fights—let them sort it out themselves.
- **Verses 10-12**
  Learn to compromise, chill out and join the party!

5. **Look over your answers for question 4. Which of those lies are you most likely to believe, and in what situation?**
Your group may have had fun answering question 4, but there's a serious point too. These lies can be subtle and are easy to swallow. Encourage them to be specific about when that might happen. The flipside of verse 7, for example, might be easy to believe in a work situation where a colleague has taken credit for your work; or in a conflict situation with extended family, perhaps it seems easiest to just tune it out rather than work for peace.

6. **In that situation, what would it look like for you to live instead like the "blessed" person Jesus describes?**
Point people back to the words of Jesus in Matthew 5:3-12 and try to apply them to the specifics of the situations people have shared.

7. **What do these verses [Matthew 5:17-20] tell us about how Christians should think about the laws of the Old Testament?**
Jesus doesn't abolish the Old Testament (v 18-19). Jesus is saying that absolutely nothing should be removed from the Old Testament. It's all part of God's revelation, and it should all be read with a corresponding seriousness.

   But Jesus does "fulfil" the Old Testament (v 17). The options are not between *abolish* and *keep-in-the-same-way*, but between *abolish* and *fulfil*. This is reflected in the repeated formula: "You have heard that it was said ... but I tell you..." (e.g. v 21-22).

   The Old Testament continues to be authoritative and relevant, but now it must be read in the light of the coming of Jesus (Luke 24:25-27, 44-47; John 5:39).
   - Sometimes Jesus fulfils the Old Testament by completing what it promised or being what it pictured.
   - Sometimes Jesus fulfils the Old Testament by affirming what it taught or deepening its meaning.

   For more on this, see *Matthew For You* p. 46-48.

8. **Fill in the table over the page. Under "practical step", identify both what Jesus says in this passage, and what an equivalent fulfilment of the heart command might look like in your modern day setting.**
You might want to split your group into smaller groups or pairs for this question, and give them one section each. The table over the page gives guidance for answers.

Explore More

- ***In each of following instances, what does the hypocrite do, and why? What is the result? What alternative does Jesus call for from his disciples?***
- ***6:2-4***
Hypocrites give publicly, and are honoured by others. But "they have received their reward in full" (v 2). People will be impressed by them.

Topic	Traditional command	Heart fulfilment	Practical step
Violence (v 21-26)	Do not murder (v 21).	Don't be angry in your hearts.	Take the initiative to settle matters quickly. E.g. don't nurse your resentment; swallow your pride, get it sorted before it escalates.
Lust (v 27-32)	Do not commit adultery (which leads to divorce).	Do not lust in your hearts—that's the real issue.	Take the initiative to avoid temptation. E.g. Turn away. Switch off. Block it. Make yourself accountable.
Suspicion and dis-honesty (v 33-37)	Do not break your oath. The Pharisees said that a vow made in God's name was binding but not a vow made "by heaven". Jesus says everything is under God's authority, so this is ridiculous reasoning and reveals a dishonest heart.	A commitment to honesty.	Earn a reputation for honesty. E.g. keep your word, meet deadlines.
Revenge (v 38-48)	"Eye for eye, and tooth for tooth" was a command to not retaliate more than you were wronged. The original aim was to limit escalating reprisals (Exodus 21:24; Leviticus 24:20; Deuteronomy 19:21). "Love your neighbour and hate your enemy" (Matthew 5:43)	"Love your enemies and pray for those persecute you" (v 44).	Take the initiative to repay with a blessing (v 39-42). E.g. pray for your enemies (v 44), greet those who are not your own people (v 47).

But that's all they get. In other words, they don't get anything from God. Instead, disciples are to give secretly, and our Father will reward us.

- ***6:5-6***
  Hypocrites pray publicly "to be seen by others". Instead, disciples are to pray in private, and our Father will reward us. NOTE: We don't need to take Jesus' words so literally that we end up being furtive. You can't contribute to a church prayer meeting in secret! But this is a good test of our motives. What we can do unseen, we should do unseen. And the key thing is that we're looking to our heavenly Father rather than looking to gauge the reaction of people on earth.

- ***6:16-18***
  Hypocrites make sure that everyone knows they are fasting. Disciples are to fast in ways that mean only God knows we're doing it, and he will reward us.

- ***7:1-5***
  Here, hypocrites boost their self-worth by putting other people down. We all have faults and struggles (specks), but the big fault (the plank) is to be self-righteous and think you're superior. The alternative is to care for one another as children of a gracious Father. Yes, we exhort people to live like Jesus (and the need for discernment is implied in verse 5). But first and foremost, we reassure believers that they're accepted in Jesus.

9. **Think over your Christian life. What evidence do you see of the law being written on your heart? How has the Spirit changed your desires and caused you to want to obey God because you love him?**
   We're right to be challenged by the Sermon on the Mount, but we have cause for gratitude too. As believers, we are not in the same position as the believers of the Old Testament; nor of the Pharisees and religious leaders of Jesus' day. We have the Spirit helping us! So, the aim of this question is to be encouraged by the ways that God is at work in us as Spirit-filled believers.

10. **How have you seen people in your church community living out the ethics and attitudes of the Sermon on the Mount in the way they treat one another?**
    This is another opportunity to encourage one another and to remember that the Sermon on the Mount is to be lived out by the Christian community. You could refer back to the Beatitudes in answering this question, as well as the commands in 5:17-48.

11. **What practical steps do you need to take to break the cycle of escalating sin?**
    This is an opportunity to look back at your answers for question 8 and identify ways in which you could put the practical steps into action in your context.

4

The King's Authority

Matthew 8:23 - 9:8; 10:1-31

The Big Idea

Jesus has the authority of God's Saviour-King to re-create the world through his words, and he entrusts that authority to his disciples, who continue and expand the mission of Jesus.

Summary

Matthew closes off the previous section of teaching with "When Jesus had finished saying these things..." (7:28). It's an echo of Genesis 2:2: "By the seventh day God had finished the work he had been doing". God created the world through his word. Now Jesus is *re*-creating the world through his words. It's a world of cleansing, welcome, healing, freedom, calm and life—one in which the threats of illness, evil, natural disaster and even death meet their match in the authority of God's Saviour-King.

Matthew gives us a glimpse of this world in chapters 8 – 9. There are ten miracle stories in these chapters—nine stories in three groups (8:1-17; 8:23 – 9:8; 9:18-34), with one story containing two miracles (v 18-26).

In this session, we'll look at the second of those three groups, where Jesus demonstrates his authority over nature (by calming the storm, 8:23-27), evil (by restoring two demon-possessed men, v 28-34), and sin and sickness (by forgiving and healing a paralysed man, 9:1-8). Jesus' authority is met with a variety of responses by the characters in the stories; ultimately, it is the crowd's awe and praise that we should seek to mirror (v 8).

The theme of authority continues into chapter 10, where Jesus shares his authority with the Twelve, giving them "authority to drive out impure spirits and to heal every disease and illness" (10:1). Their message is to be his message (v 7; 4:17). In other words, the disciples are to continue and expand the mission of Jesus.

This is a chapter with lessons for contemporary mission. But not everything here applies today because this missionary campaign belonged to a specific moment in the story of salvation. The disciples are to go only to towns in Israel (10:6-8). The time for Gentile mission will come (28:18-20), but for now, Israel is the priority. As Jesus prepares to head to Jerusalem, he's giving Israel as a nation an opportunity to acknowledge him as their national Messiah.

The disciples are warned of the prospect of rejection (10:12-24) but are assured of God's fatherly care and that ultimately the church's mission will succeed (v 24-31). As believers living on the other side of the sending of the Spirit at Pentecost, we too can be encouraged in our evangelism by these promises.

Optional Extra

After reading about Jesus sending the Twelve on mission in Matthew 10, end your study with an extended time of prayer for one or more of your church's mission partners. Print out their most recent newsletter or prayer requests to share with the group, and email your mission partner afterwards to let them know you've been praying. If security considerations permit, you could even record part of your prayer time as audio or send a short video message from your group with your greetings.

Guidance for Questions

1. **What's your idea of a perfect world? If you were redesigning the world from scratch, what would you change?**
   Your group may want to have some fun with this! It links to the idea that Jesus' miracles demonstrate how he is *re*-creating the world through his words. It's a world of cleansing, welcome, healing, freedom, calm and life—one in which the threats of illness, evil, natural disaster and even death meet their match in the authority of God's Saviour-King.

2. **What does Jesus demonstrate his authority over in 8:23-27, and how?**
   Jesus demonstrates his authority over nature. With a word, Jesus commands a storm, "and it was completely calm" (v 26). Matthew uses the word "rebuke". I can rebuke my children because I have authority over them. But if I tried to rebuke a stranger, I would be considered a ranting madman! That Jesus rebukes the storm is a sign of his authority as God's King; that the storm obeys only reinforces this.

   - **How do people respond to his authority?**
     The story ends with the disciples asking, "What kind of man is this?" (v 27). It's the question Matthew poses to us. What do *you* make of Jesus? Who do you think he is? It's a question that will be answered in 16:16, but along the way, Matthew is giving us plenty of clues. Here he (uniquely) records the disciples crying out, "Save us!" (10:25). Jesus can save people from a storm—but Matthew wants us to wonder whether Jesus can save us from more than this.

3. **What does Jesus demonstrate his authority over in verses 28-34, and how?**
   Jesus demonstrates his authority over the spiritual world. Both the physical and spiritual worlds were created through Jesus and are subject to his power. The interaction with the herd of pigs highlights this; the demons can only act with his permission.

   - **How do people respond to his authority?**
     It's too much for the townsfolk. They beg Jesus to leave just as the demons begged Jesus to be allowed to leave. ("Begged" and "pleaded" in verses 31 and 34 of the NIV translation are the same word in the original Greek.)

4. **What does Jesus demonstrate his authority over in 9:1-8, and how?**
   Jesus demonstrates his authority to forgive sin. Forgiving sin is God's prerogative. So for Jesus to declare the man forgiven is to act as God—and that's blasphemy (v 3): unless, of course, Jesus really is Immanuel, God with us. So he demonstrates his authority over sin by demonstrating his authority over sickness, which is a physical manifestation of sin's impact on humanity (v 5).

- **How do people respond to his authority?**
  The paralysed man gets up and walks; he demonstrates faith in Jesus' power. The teachers of the law bridle at Jesus' assertion of authority; as Matthew's Gospel continues, their rejection of Jesus will continue to harden. The crowd exemplify how we should respond: we should praise God for giving this authority to Jesus (v 8).

5. **What do these three stories tell us about the re-created world that Jesus is bringing about? Why is that good news for you this week?**
   Matthew is inviting us to see these incidents from the life of Jesus as a foretaste of God's coming salvation. God is going to recreate the world. In this new creation, the forces of nature will no longer be a threat (the chaotic sea of Matthew 8:24 will be no more, according to Revelation 21:1), evil spirits will have been defeated, and sin and sickness will be gone for ever. The miracles of Jesus are the promise of a world made new for all who turn to him in faith. This is great news for us as we persevere in faith amid chaos, evil, suffering and sin. Encourage your group to share ways in which this particularly encourages them in their present circumstances.

6. **Look back at the different responses to Jesus' authority in these three stories. Have you observed people responding in similar ways to Jesus' authoritative claims when they encounter the gospel message? How?**
   A key part of the gospel message is that Jesus is the rightful King of the world, and becoming a Christian involves submitting to his authority over our lives. When the gospel is preached, it will be met with different responses. Some people are curious, like the disciples in the boat; others are fearful of the implications that his claims would have on their lives, and politely decline the offer, like the townspeople; some are indignant, like the teachers of the law; and others still will respond with faith, awe and praise.

7. **Which of the responses in this passage do you think we should be seeking to mirror? What would that look like for you tomorrow?**
   The crowd in 9:8 exemplify how we should respond: we should praise God for giving this authority to Jesus.

Explore More

- ***What does this incident [in Matthew 9:9-13] teach us about Jesus' mission? Why is this good news for us?***
  Welcoming sinners is central to Jesus' mission: "I have not come to call the righteous, but sinners" (v 13). It would be crazy for a doctor to refuse to treat the sick because she disapproved of sickness! Physically sick people need a doctor, and spiritually sick people need Jesus (v 12). This is good news for us, because we are all spiritually sick sinners. The reason why Pharisees don't come to Jesus is not because they're genuinely righteous but because they won't acknowledge their need.

- ***Who might be the equivalent of "tax collectors" in your world? Would you be delighted to see them receive God's blessing of salvation? Or would you be shocked that they should so easily be forgiven?***
  Today, the equivalent might be addicts, or prodigals who were raised in the faith, lived wildly and then returned. Or there might be groups specific to your context that people can think of.

- ***Matthew tells his story and opens his home to share Jesus with others. How could you do that this month?***
  Telling the story of how Jesus has saved us and changed us is a powerful way of sharing the gospel. The key thing is to ensure that the spotlight falls on Jesus and his grace. We need to ensure that our story nestles within Christ's story. Encourage your group to think about how you could tell Christ's story by telling your story, and to whom. Our meals, too, can be part of the mission of Jesus as we embody God's grace in the welcome we extend to those in need. Like Matthew, we can invite people to meet Jesus around the table.

---

8. **Where does Jesus tell the Twelve to go (v 5-6)?**
   Jesus sends the Twelve "to the lost sheep of Israel" (v 6)—"the sheep without a shepherd" of 9:36. As Jesus prepares to head to Jerusalem, he's giving Israel as a nation an opportunity to acknowledge him as their national Messiah. Why are the Gentiles excluded, especially when Jesus himself has already healed the servant of a Gentile centurion and visited a Gentile region (8:13, 28)? The answer is that the time for Gentile mission will come (28:18-20), but for now, Israel is the priority.

- **What are they told to do (v 7-8), and how are they going to do it (v 1)?**
  Jesus has been "healing every disease and illness" (9:35). Now he gives his disciples "authority to drive out impure spirits and to heal every disease and illness" (10:1). Their message is to be his message (v 7; 4:17). In other words, the disciples are to continue and expand the

mission of Jesus. They're to pass on what they've received because the blessing of Jesus is not divided when shared—it is multiplied (10:8).

9. **Why might the disciples have cause to be afraid at this assignment (v 14-25)?**
   Matthew 10:11-13 implies that the disciples have a reasonable prospect of a warm welcome in some locations. But verses 13-15 suggest this will not always be the case, and the prospect of rejection comes to the fore in the remainder of the chapter. The disciples may have authority over spirits and sickness (v 1), but this doesn't make them immune to suffering. While verses 17-20 apply to the temporary mission to ethnic Israel upon which the disciples are about to embark, they seem to look beyond this to the ongoing mission of the church. There's no indication that the Twelve were brought before "governors and kings" at this stage, and they've been explicitly told to avoid "Gentiles" (compare v 18). But in time, they will certainly face the persecution Jesus describes.

10. **Why don't they need to be afraid, according to Jesus?**
    - **Verses 18-20**
      Because the Spirit will speak through them. This is true of all evangelism (see 2 Corinthians 5:20). But it's particularly helpful to remember this when we're defending our faith in a hostile context (Matthew 10:19-20). Jesus describes the Holy Spirit as "the Spirit of your Father" (v 20). It's a lovely reminder that believers are part of the divine family, with God as our Father and Jesus as our brother.
    - **Verses 26-27**
      Because the message will be heard. What Jesus speaks in private is what the disciples will declare publicly. Despite all opposition, the message of Jesus will spread. No matter what the world throws at the church, our mission will succeed.
    - **Verses 28-31**
      Because we're in God's care, now and for ever. While verse 28 is not saying that the soul is more important than the body, it is saying that eternal life is more important than our present, temporary lives. So don't fear those who can destroy your physical body (merely taking away this temporary life); instead fear the one who can destroy your spiritual self (taking away eternal life)—except you don't need to fear this one because he's "your Father", and *you will not fall to the ground outside his care* (v 29). The hostility may not go away, and it could even end in death. But God is in every detail (v 30), you are precious to him (v 31), and he will bring you safely home to glory.

11. **What are your fears when it comes to evangelism?**
    Often, we worry that we'll cause offence or be rejected, or that our efforts won't work, so it's not worth the effort.

12. **How does what we've read speak into those fears?**
    When mission goes badly, it's easy to assume the problem is with us, and it's good to ask whether we've been insensitive or arrogant. But more often, our message is rejected through no fault of our own. Jesus prepares us for opposition so that when it comes, we're not alarmed or disturbed. Instead, we can take comfort in God's care (v 28-31) and have confidence that as the message goes out, some will hear it and welcome it (v 11).

5

The Kingdom Resisted

Matthew 12:1-14; 13:24-46

The Big Idea

Jesus' kingdom may be resisted and rejected—but it is coming now in grace and will one day come in glory.

Summary

Jesus has come to renew God's people and establish God's kingdom. We've seen his authority over both the physical and spiritual worlds. All seems to be going well. However, there have been a few hints that opposition is possible (5:10-12; 9:3, 34; 10:16-39)—and in chapter 11, that opposition becomes a reality. Then in chapter 12, it continues to intensify.

The first part of this session looks at the first of Jesus' major run-ins with the Pharisees, regarding the observance of the Sabbath (12:1-14). This picks up the theme of rest from 11:28-30 (see Getting Personal on page 37). But the wider theme of opposition also remains. The Pharisees question Jesus in 12:2; look for reasons to charge him in verse 10; and plot his death in verse 14. The Law of Moses spelt out for the Israelites what it meant to love God and people in a host of different situations. But the Pharisees made these stipulations an end in themselves rather than seeing how they shaped love for others. In contrast, Jesus offers true rest to the overburdened (Matthew 11:28). As the Lord of the Sabbath, Jesus keeps the Sabbath regulations in a richer, deeper way.

The second part of this session covers some of the parables of the kingdom from chapter 13. Matthew 13 begins, "That same day..." (v 1), tying what follows with the day of disputes in Matthew 12. Is Jesus God's King establishing God's kingdom? If so, where's the defeat of God's enemies? Jesus responds to these questions by telling a series of parables about the kingdom of heaven. As the note in the study guide explains, each parable reinforces the "secrets" of the kingdom: that is, that it comes in two stages—first in grace and finally in glory. The parables protect this secret by revealing the truth to some and keeping it concealed from others. They genuinely announce the coming of the kingdom, but they do so in a way that enlightens the soft-hearted while hiding the truth from those hardened in unbelief (13:12-13). The key idea is that…

- the kingdom *will come* in power as expected; there will be a day of judgment.
- the kingdom *has already come* in a hidden way: as a gracious invitation to receive forgiveness before it's too late.

These parables encourage us in our witness when the church feels weak and insignificant.

Optional Extra

After question 7 or 8, write your own contemporary parables that express the two secrets of the kingdom. (Or set this as a "homework" activity and then feed back at the start of your next session, by way of recap.)

Guidance for Questions

1. **Describe your typical Sunday.**
   Hopefully, attending church will be a common feature! But what do members of your group do before that and afterwards? Do they have traditions, routines or rules that make Sunday different from other days? Why do they do those things? In this study we'll look at some of Jesus' teaching on the Sabbath and consider what principles it might give us for how we spend our Sundays.

2. **How do we see the Pharisees' opposition to Jesus escalate over the course of this episode?**

- **Verse 2**
  They start with an accusation. The Pharisees challenge Jesus because his disciples pick ears of corn on the Sabbath (v 1-2). But the disciples are not bringing in the harvest—just picking a few grains to eat as they walk along (much as people in the UK might pick blackberries on a Sunday afternoon walk).

- **Verse 10**
  Now they go one further and seek to provoke a reaction. Matthew tells us they are "looking for a reason to bring charges against Jesus" (v 10). They clearly think it would be wrong for Jesus to heal the man because this would constitute working on the Sabbath.

- **Verse 14**
  Now they are plotting to kill Jesus. The contrast with Jesus is stark. The Pharisees work towards death on the Sabbath because Jesus has worked life on the Sabbath.

3. **What do we learn here about what God intended the Sabbath for?**

- **Matthew 12:7**
  Jesus quotes Hosea 6:6: "I desire mercy, not sacrifice". God wants people to pursue the goal of the law (which is love) rather than simply tick religious boxes. The Sabbath was a gift to people oppressed by overwork (as former slaves in Egypt in the first instance), but the Pharisees had made it another burden. In contrast, Jesus offers true rest to the overburdened (Matthew 11:28, see Getting Personal).

- **Verses 11-13**
  Jesus highlights the Pharisees' hypocrisy—they would rescue a sheep on the Sabbath (giving a kind of Sabbath rest to a distressed animal), yet a person is worth far more than a sheep (v 11-12). They can flex the law when it suits them (by saving a stuck sheep) but won't show the love commended by the law. So Jesus heals the man (v 13), bringing healing, rest and life, as the Sabbath was intended to do. The Lord of the Sabbath keeps the Sabbath in a richer, deeper way.

4. **Why does Jesus have the right to say what the law truly means (v 6, 8)?**
   Jesus says, "I tell you that something greater than the temple is here … For the Son of Man is Lord of the Sabbath" (v 6, 8). That "something greater" is Jesus himself. Jesus is the true temple: the "place" in whom we meet God and come to be cleansed. Jesus can interpret the law because he is the law-giver. He is the one who spoke to Moses at Mount Sinai, and he is the one who has given a new law to a new people on a new mount in Matthew 5 – 7. Jesus himself is the true Sabbath, in whom we find rest (11:28).

5. **Does the way you use your Sunday bring rest, or is it a burden? What could you do differently?**
   Refer back to your group's answers to question 1. Do people use their Sundays in ways that help them to enjoy rest in Jesus? Christians hold a variety of positions about how the Sabbath applies today and what requirements the New Testament places on believers with regards to the Lord's Day, and there may be a wide range of views in your group. This is an area over which Christians ought to avoid judging one another (Romans 14:5-8).

6. **How could you use your Sunday to bring rest to, or relieve the burdens of, someone in your church family?**
   We can bring rest to others as we serve at church in ways that enable them to hear the words of Jesus—whether that's serving on the tech team or volunteering in the kids' ministry. We can relieve burdens as we chat with brothers and sisters over coffee, by asking thoughtful questions, listening to their answers, speaking of Jesus and praying together. We can relieve the burden of loneliness by showing hospitality

and providing space for fellowship. (For some, Sunday can be the loneliest day of the week.) Perhaps we could use Sunday afternoon to do some jobs around the house for an older member of our church family who is less able to do these things themselves.

7. **Look at the parables of the mustard seed and the yeast (v 31-33). How do they reveal the two secrets of the kingdom?**
   Both these parables involve something small—"the smallest of all seeds" and hidden yeast. (In verse 33, "mixed" is literally "hid" in the flour, ESV.) But in both cases, they become something big—"the largest of garden plants" and something working "all through the dough" (v 31-33).

- **The kingdom is coming in grace.** The kingdom *is coming* now in grace, even though at the moment it looks very small. Don't be misled by that smallness; God is doing a new thing in history (v 35).

- **The kingdom will come in glory.** The birds perching in the tree's branches is a picture of people from all nations finding refuge under Christ's rule (v 32).

8. **Look at the parable of the weeds (v 24-30, 36-43). How does it reveal the two secrets of the kingdom?**
   Jesus tells the parable of a field in which an enemy sows weeds among the wheat. Rather than risk pulling up wheat plants, the owner tells his servants to wait and divide the wheat and weeds at harvest time (v 29-30). (The parable of the net makes the same point, using good and bad fish in a net, in verses 47-49.)

- **The kingdom is coming in grace.** The kingdom *is coming* now, even though judgment (the division of wheat and weeds and the division of bad and good fish) has been delayed. It's coming in grace as the word is proclaimed.

- **The kingdom will come in glory.** There will be a harvest at the end of the age (v 40-41). So don't be fooled: just because the kingdom comes now in grace doesn't mean judgment has been permanently cancelled.

9. **Look at the parables of the treasure and the pearl (v 44-46). How do these prompt us to respond to the secrets of the kingdom, and why?**
   Both people in these parables sell all they own to gain a treasure—and both gain something they consider far more valuable. These parables are beautiful pictures of the way that those who lose their life for Christ's sake actually find it (10:38-39; 16:24-27) and those who reject treasure on earth gain treasure in heaven (6:19-20). Notice, too, how the first man sold all he had "in his joy" (13:44). This future hope—that God's kingdom will come in glory—enables us to rejoice even when we're making sacrifices or when serving Jesus is hard going.

Explore More

- ***How does the parable of the sower reveal the two secrets of the kingdom?***

  The kingdom expands whenever people hear its message and submit to the authority of the King in repentance. The kingdom is coming largely unseen as the seed is sown through the proclamation of the gospel, and the kingdom will come in the form of a great harvest (a common image in the Bible for the final judgment). The word of the kingdom may be rejected, neglected and opposed, but it's also growing and producing fruit.

- ***What does this parable suggest we should expect to happen as people hear the message of the kingdom?***

  The focus of the parable of the sower is on the mixed response to the message. It illustrates the reason why Jesus speaks in parables—to both reveal and conceal the good news. So the parable of the sower is a parable about parables!

  The path = an immediate rejection. Some people immediately dismiss the message (v 19), either through hostility or apathy. Jesus attributes this to the work of Satan. Such people may come to church out of habit or with their family. They should beware. The more they hear, the less impact it has (v 13).

  The rocky soil = a superficial response. These people respond enthusiastically. They like what they hear. Perhaps they are moved by the eloquence or passion of the speaker. But any profession of faith is merely an emotional response. They haven't counted the cost. So, "when trouble or persecution comes because of the word, they quickly fall away" (v 20-21).

  The thorns = a divided heart. These people may show some initial interest, but they're soon distracted by worldly cares and attractions (v 22).

  The good soil = a fruitful transformation. The kingdom may not be advanced by force in the sense of coercion, but the preaching of the kingdom has the power to change and transform. It's not merely an ideology that inspires; it's a word that brings life and bears fruit.

- ***How does this parable encourage us as we seek to share the message of the kingdom?***

  We shouldn't be surprised or disheartened when we're rejected—this is normal. Some Christians assume the problem is with the seed; they think the gospel message needs to be updated for a contemporary audience. But there's nothing wrong with the seed in the parable; the problem is with the soil. So what do we do? We keep on sowing. This parable is a call to persevere. The story doesn't end with barren land; the story ends with a harvest.

10. Based on these parables, what would you say to...

- **an older person in your church**

family who says, "Things were so much better when I was young. The church had real influence in our culture back then. Now things are going downhill."

The true church usually seems weak and insignificant. These parables tell us to expect that. Yet somehow the gospel has spread across the globe! You may feel you have little to offer, or that the church's influence in the culture has waned. Perhaps you're right! But look at what God can do with a little (v 31-33)! He is growing his kingdom in quiet ways we can't always see.

- **a younger person in your church family who says, "My friends think Christianity is an absolute joke. I'm not sure following Jesus is worth the grief I get. They seem to get on fine without him."**

The parables of the hidden treasure and the pearl remind us that following Jesus is costly but ultimately worth it. For now, the wheat and the weeds stand side by side, and belonging to Jesus doesn't always seem to place us at an advantage—sometimes it does the opposite. But a harvest is coming, and we'd be foolish to walk away from Jesus before then.

6

Peter's Hits and Misses

Matthew 14:22-36; 16:13-28

The Big Idea

Jesus is the Messiah, the Son of the living God and the "I Am" himself, who will suffer and die in our place. We must respond in faith and follow him.

Summary

This section (Matthew 14 – 16) centres around two key questions: "Who is Jesus?" and "How will you respond to him?" It climaxes with Jesus being acclaimed as "the Messiah, the Son of the living God" (16:16).

As we move towards that moment, we see examples of faith and unbelief. We'll focus on 14:22-36. The disciples are in the middle of a storm when Jesus walks on the water towards them (v 22-25: an image associated in the Old Testament with Yahweh himself). They assume he's a ghost, but his words reassure them (v 26-27). Jesus climbs into the boat, and the storm dies down (v 32), but not before Peter is invited to walk on the water (v 28-29). It's a great step of faith (literally). But when Peter sees the wind, he begins to sink, and so Jesus has to grab hold of him (v 30-31). As we build up to the confession of 16:16, Peter illustrates the current state of the disciples: wavering between belief and unbelief. This is why Jesus responds, "You of little faith … why did you doubt?" (14:31). (The Explore More takes in the contrasting example of the Canaanite woman's persevering faith in 15:21-28.)

Like Peter, we're to walk through the storms of life by faith and not by sight, by fixing our attention on the word of Jesus rather than looking at the threats and seductions of this world. Our faith may fail as Peter's does, but Jesus remains faithful. Jesus will catch hold of us when we fall (14:31).

In the second half of the study, we'll jump ahead to 16:13-28, where the disciples finally recognise Jesus as the Messiah in verses 13-20. Even at this point, though, they are only halfway to a proper understanding of Jesus, and so Jesus must begin to explain what being the Messiah actually involves (v 21-28). The Jews expected the Messiah to judge God's enemies (as we saw in Matthew 13), and Jesus confirms this expectation in 16:27. But first, the Messiah must die a violent death (v 21). He "must" be killed if we're to be saved (v 21).

Indeed, not only must Jesus accept death, but so must his disciples. If verse 16 summarises who Jesus is, verse 24 summarises what it means to follow him: "Whoever wants to be my disciple must deny themselves and take up their cross and follow me". It's a big demand. But Jesus promises it is worth it.

Optional Extra

To bring the reading of Matthew 14:22-36 to life, play some storm sounds in the background as you read. (Fade them out after verse 32.)

Guidance for Questions

1. **Imagine a non-Christian friend asks you, "So, who exactly was this Jesus you Christians go on about?" How would you answer?**
   The question "Who is Jesus?" is key to this section of Matthew's Gospel. We'll return to this question at the end of the study.

2. **We've already seen the disciples in a boat in rough weather (8:23-27). What is similar about this encounter? What's different this time?**
   The obvious difference is the walking-on-water incident, to which we return in question 4. Similarities include how, in both encounters, Jesus can calm the waters (8:26; 14:32). In Matthew 8, Jesus questions the "little faith" of his disciples (8:26), and in 14:31 he questions the faith of Peter in the same way. But there are signs of a deepened understanding of who Jesus is. When Jesus calmed the storm in 8:23-27, the disciples asked, "What kind of *man* is this?" (v 27). Now, as Jesus again calms a storm, they answer their own question: "Truly you are the Son of God" (14:33).

3. **This passage is rich with allusions to the Old Testament. Read Job 9:8,**

Isaiah 43:1-2 and Exodus 3:13-14. In light of these passages, what is Matthew telling us about who Jesus is, do you think? (Note that when Jesus says "It is I" in verse 27, it is literally "I am".)

- In Job 9:8, God treads on the waves. So, Jesus walking on water is an allusion to his divinity.
- Water in the Bible often serves as a picture of judgment. But just as in Isaiah God says, "Do not fear" (Isaiah 43:1), so here Jesus says, "Don't be afraid" (Matthew 14:27). In Isaiah God promises, "I will be with you"—and Jesus is Immanuel, coming through the storm to his people.
- At the burning bush, Moses asked, *What is your name?* and God replied, "I AM WHO I AM" (Exodus 3:14). Now, as Jesus comes to his disciples, he says, "It is I" (literally "I am"). He is God—but God come close. Moses was warned not to come too close to the burning bush; and later in Exodus, when "I am" came down to his people at Mount Sinai, a barrier was placed round the mountain, and God was hidden in cloud because God and humanity couldn't safely live together (19:9, 12-13). But now, Immanuel steps down from the mountain (Matthew 14:23) and comes to meet us in the storms of life (v 25). You and Jesus are in the same boat.

4. **Matthew is the only Gospel to include the story of Peter walking on the water. What do you think Matthew wants us to learn from it?**
    - As we build up to the confession of 16:16, Peter illustrates the current state of the disciples: wavering between belief and unbelief. This is why Jesus responds, "You of little faith ... why did you doubt?" (14:31).
    - The story serves as a model of faith for God's people in any age. Peter walked on water when he trusted the word of Jesus (v 29); he began to sink "when he saw the wind" (v 30). Likewise, we're to walk through the storms of life by faith and not by sight, by fixing our attention on the word of Jesus rather than looking at the threats and seductions of this world.
    - Beneath our faith is a greater faith. Our faith may fail as Peter's does, but Jesus remains faithful. Jesus will catch hold of us when we fall (v 31). Here, Peter prefigures his fall in 26:69-75—a fall from which Jesus will ultimately lift him.

Explore More

- ***Read Matthew 15:21-28. Where is this woman from (v 21-22), and why is that significant?***
  She is a Canaanite and therefore not a Jew but a pagan. Jewish people did not regard Canaanites as trustworthy. Moreover, alert readers will still have in mind John's defeat at the hands of Herodias, a new Jezebel (14:1-12). Jezebel was a princess from

Sidon (1 Kings 16:31)—and here we meet another woman from Sidon. It doesn't bode well.

- ***Given that, what is surprising about who she says Jesus is (v 22)?***
  She says that Jesus is the "Son of David" (v 22). This pagan woman acknowledges Jesus as the promised Davidic Messiah before the disciples! In 12:23, the crowd asked, "Could this be the Son of David?" but the only other people to acknowledge Jesus as the Son of David have been two blind men (9:27; see also 20:30-31). The irony is that it's the blind who recognise Jesus and Gentiles who acknowledge him as Israel's King.

- ***Jesus says that she has "great faith" (v 28). How do we see that in her conversation with Jesus (v 22-27)? Why do you think Jesus rebuffs her three times?***
  Three times she's rebuffed, and three times she persists. At first, Jesus' attitude seems harsh and uncaring. But "cold print does not allow us to detect a quizzical eyebrow or a tongue in the cheek, and it may be that Jesus' demeanour already hinted that his discouraging reply was not to be his last word on the subject" (R.T. France, *The Gospel of Matthew*, New International Commentary on the New Testament (Eerdmans, 2007), p. 591). *Certainly, in hindsight, it's clear that Jesus was pushing her with the intention of revealing the depth of her faith. Jesus ignored her so he might commend her. He rebuffed her so she might become a model of persistent faith (in contrast with the disciples' "little faith").*

---

5. **What is the "wind" that you're tempted to look at and become fearful of? What gives you that sinking feeling?**
   The potential answers to this question are as varied as the members of your group!

6. **How can we help one another to fix our eyes on Jesus when walking through the storms of life? Be specific. (Perhaps try helping one another to look to Jesus in your fears right now!)**
   Helping one another to fix our eyes on Jesus will certainly involve praying with and for one another; it will require being honest about ways in which we're struggling; and it will call for brothers and sisters to speak gentle words about Jesus in times of fear—perhaps a simple story about him from the Gospels that speaks to his character. (We could even start with this one.) Sometimes we're wary of doing this because we're fearful of sounding trite or getting it wrong. But even the most fumbling words—when true and spoken in love from the heart—can be powerful.

7. **What does Peter now believe about who Jesus is (v 16)?**
   Peter says, "You are the Messiah, the Son of the living God". This is a central moment in Matthew's story

because this is his core message. Jesus is God's King, come to rescue God's people from judgment and restore God's life-giving rule. Indeed, Jesus is God himself, Immanuel, God with us.

8. **So why does Peter "get it" now, according to Jesus (v 17)?**
Jesus says, "Blessed are you, Simon [Peter] son of Jonah, for this was not revealed to you by flesh and blood, but by my Father in heaven". None of us is a Christian because we were clever enough to work it out. Faith is always a gift from God, given through the regenerating work of the Holy Spirit (John 3:3-6; Ephesians 2:8).

9. **What has Peter misunderstood about what it means for Jesus to be the Messiah?**
"From that time on" in verse 21 marks a new stage in Jesus' ministry. Now that the disciples have recognised him as the Messiah, he moves on to Lesson 2: what does it mean to be the Messiah? The Jews expected the Messiah to judge God's enemies (as we saw in Matthew 13), and Jesus confirms this expectation in 16:27. But first, the Messiah must die a violent death (v 21). It's Jesus who's going to be judged—not for his own rebellion but for ours. He "must" be killed if we're to be saved (v 21)—otherwise his coming in judgment will mean our condemnation. Defeat and death are not on Peter's agenda, however, and so he rebukes Jesus (v 22). Jesus interprets this as a temptation from Satan to avoid the agonies of the cross (v 23; 4:8-9). A moment before, Peter was a foundation stone; now he's "a stumbling-block".

10. **What does Jesus say about what it means for us to be his disciples?**
If verse 16 summarises who Jesus is, verse 24 summarises what it means to follow him. We're to show the same submission to God, willingness to serve and sacrificial love that Jesus displayed at the cross. For some, this may mean martyrdom; for all, it means dying to our proud, selfish self. To deny ourselves (v 24) doesn't mean we should always default to saying no to what we want. The only other time the word "denial" is used in Matthew's Gospel is to describe Peter's denial of Jesus (26:34-35, 75—"disown" is the same word in the Greek). For Peter, denying Jesus meant not being identified by his allegiance to Jesus. Denying self means not finding our identity in our accomplishments but instead finding it in Jesus, and putting our allegiance to him first.

- **It's a big demand. Is it worth it?**
Yes, because those who lose their life for Jesus will find it (v 25); they will be rewarded when Jesus returns (v 27). But how can we be sure? Because Jesus' transfiguration, resurrection and ascension, and the spread of the gospel are indications that Jesus has *already* conquered. We're on the winning side!

NOTE: Some members of your group may have questions about

what verse 28 means. Jesus didn't mistakenly think history would end in the 1st century AD. The point is that the victory of Jesus had a number of major anticipatory events coming up, which some of his hearers would witness:

- The transfiguration of Jesus, when Peter, James and John were given a glimpse of his future glory (17:1-8).
- The resurrection of Jesus, when he rose in triumph (28:2-4).
- The ascension of Jesus, when he came before God to receive all authority (Daniel 7:13-14).
- The fall of Jerusalem in AD 70, when Jesus was vindicated (see Matthew 24:1-35).
- The expansion of the kingdom of Jesus to all nations through the mission of the church (28:18-20).

11. **In question 1, we imagined a non-Christian friend asking, "So, who exactly was this Jesus you Christians go on about?" How would you answer now, in light of this study?**

    Take the truths we've considered and see if you can express them in a way that someone completely unfamiliar with Christianity would understand. Your group might enjoy doing this as a role play in pairs. Perhaps we'd say something like "Jesus was a real person who lived in Israel in the 1st century. But he was more than that, too; he was the Son of God, come down to earth. He lived and died and rose again, and he's still alive today. We've all chosen to reject God's rule over our lives. That's what the Bible calls sin. But Jesus came to rescue people from their sin and invite them to live under his good rule."

- **How would you explain to them what it means to be a Christian, based on the truths we've considered in these verses?**

  Perhaps we'd say something like "To be a Christian is to be a follower of Jesus. It means that you acknowledge that he is who he said he is: not just a wise guru or a figure from history but God's Son and the rightful ruler of our lives. And it means he becomes your highest allegiance—even if that means doing difficult things, as he did."

7

The First, Last and the Last, First

Matthew 20:1-16; 21:1-32

The Big Idea

Jesus is the humble king who came to bring peace. Those who humbly receive his generosity are welcomed into his kingdom; but those who are self-righteous and refuse to repent will be excluded.

Summary

In chapter 19 Matthew introduced a group of children and a rich man. Of those two parties, who's done more for God? Who's spent more time in prayer? Who's given more donations? Who's studied the Scriptures the most? The answer is clearly the rich man. Yet we end up with the little children being blessed in God's kingdom (19:15) and the rich man walking away sad (v 22). The chapter ends, "But many who are first will be last, and many who are last will be first", and a similar phrase concludes the next parable (20:16).

The parable (v 1-16) tells the story of a landowner who hires day-labourers to gather his harvest (v 1). Some workers are hired early in the morning, and so they work all day (v 2); others are hired later and only work part of the day (v 3-7). Yet all end up being paid the same wage (v 8-10). The all-day workers grumble at this (v 11-12). But they receive their agreed wage (v 13-14). The point is that no one earns their way into the kingdom of Jesus. It's those who *become* like dependent children who enter the kingdom and those who *live* like dependent children who are great in the kingdom (see 18:3-4).

The theme of the upside-down authority of Jesus continues with the next story in this session: the triumphal entry into Jerusalem (21:1-11). While the donkey is a symbol of messianic authority, the connection with Zechariah (v 5) spotlights that King Jesus is not a normal king. He's not coming to conquer Jerusalem but to bring peace.

The final part of the study shows the first becoming last as Jesus drives the money-changers from the temple and curses a fig tree as an enacted parable against the fruitless temple and the religious symbol it represented (v 12-19).

This is once more underlined in a parable (v 28-32). A man asks his two sons to work in his vineyard. One son says he won't serve but does, while the other says he will serve but doesn't. Similarly, at the start of their lives, the tax collectors and prostitutes looked like people who refused to serve God, but now they're repenting of their sin and entering the kingdom through faith (v 31-32). The religious leaders, on the other hand, proclaimed their obedience but then refused to listen to God's prophet—Jesus (v 32). The religious leaders saw themselves as custodians of the temple, but the house of prayer is being reassigned to repentant sinners. The first will be last, and the last will be first.

Optional Extra

For a not too serious introduction to the theme of "The first will be last, and the last will be first", watch a clip of Australian speed skater Steven Bradbury winning gold in the 1,000m event at the 2002 Winter Olympics: www.youtube.com/watch?v=WUi4-H6hfw8.

Guidance for Questions

1. **Think of some examples of the last coming first or the first coming last—great sporting comebacks or failures, unlikely victories or defeats from history, or unexpected reversals of fortune from books or films.**
   Potential examples could include: Liverpool winning the 2005 UEFA Champions League final, coming back from 3-0 down at half-time; the English victory at Agincourt in 1415; Sam and Frodo's role in defeating Sauron in *The Lord of the Rings*.

2. **Retell the parable in your own words.**
   A landowner hires day-labourers to gather his harvest (v 1). Some workers are hired early in the morning, and so they work all day (v 2). At different points in the day, other workers are hired, who then only work part of the day (v 3-7). Yet all end up being paid the same wage (v 8-10). The all-day workers grumble at this (v 11-12). But they receive their agreed wage (v 13-14). *Why are you complaining?* says the landowner. *Can't I do what I want with my own money? Or are you jealous of my generosity?* (v 15).

3. **Who are "the first" in this parable, and what do they end up with? Who are "the last", and what do they end up with?**
   "The first" are those who were hired at the start of the day. They end up with a denarius. "The last" are those who were hired at the end of the day. They end up with a denarius too.

- **Are the workers who were hired early hard done by? Why, or why not?**
  No—they got the wage they deserved. It's just that the ones who were hired late in the day got more than they deserved. We may identify with the indignance of "the first" workers. But as the owner says, "Don't I have the right to do what I want with my own money?"

4. **What do you think this story is telling us about the kingdom of Jesus?**
   The parable begins and ends with the reversal of the first and last (19:30; 20:16), suggesting that it's a commentary on the whole of Matthew 18 – 19, and especially the inclusion of "little ones" and "little children" (18:2-6, 10; 19:13-15)

and the self-exclusion of the rich man (v 22). The point is that no one earns their way into the kingdom of Jesus, and no one gains extra status through their good works. So when it comes to receiving blessing from God, we shouldn't be surprised if those blessings don't correlate with the merit of the recipient. God's generous grace doesn't work like that. That's just as well, for if we received what we deserved, we'd all be in deep trouble. But God, in his love, blesses us far above and beyond our merits.

5. **When might we be tempted to begrudge God's generosity to others?**
   Often it's when he blesses them with the things we want but don't have: a spouse, a child, a promotion, a big house, or children who follow Jesus into adulthood. Perhaps someone we grew up with embraced a wild lifestyle before coming to faith later in life—and we begrudge the fact that it could be so easy. Or maybe we watch on as God blesses other churches which appear less faithful than ours, and we begrudge their growth.

6. **What might that reveal about our view of the following? And in each case, what would the right view be instead?**

- **Ourselves**
  It might reveal that we feel we deserve God's blessing. We think we've earned it when, in fact, we haven't.

- **God**
  It might reveal that we think God is stingy or unfair. But, as Matt Searles puts it, this is "a wrong view of God. The true antidote to entitlement is to understand the character of God: like the vineyard owner he is generous and loves to give good things. He never gives less than anyone deserves, but he delights to give more!" (*Matthew: One Greater Than Solomon* (10Publishing, 2018), p. 32)

- **The kingdom**
  It might reveal that we think that growth in God's kingdom, or our part in it, should correlate with the effort we put in. But no one enters the kingdom through their good works. It's those who become like dependent children who enter the kingdom and those who live like dependent children who are great in the kingdom (18:3-4).

7. **What is surprising about Jesus' choice of transportation?**
   A donkey is an unassuming sort of animal. In Zechariah 9 they're contrasted to the enemy's "chariots" and "war-horses". Imagine a rider on a donkey tilting into battle against a mighty stallion! But King Jesus is not a normal king.

- **What is significant about it? What does it reveal about who he is, and what he's come to do?**
  Matthew quotes Zechariah 9:9-10, which speaks of the coming of a king who will proclaim peace to the nations.

By entering Jerusalem on a donkey, Jesus was claiming to be God's promised King (Matthew 21:6-8).

But donkeys were also a sign of peace. Jesus was not coming to conquer Jerusalem but to bring peace. As Matt Searles puts it, Jesus is "showing what sort of king he is. There is no horse, no chariot, no show of power or strength. Jesus is a humble king." (Searles, *Matthew*, p. 34)

8. **Who does Jesus expel *out* of the temple, and why? Who does he welcome *in*?**
When someone made a pilgrimage to the temple, they needed both an animal to sacrifice and to convert their Roman money into the temple currency in order to pay the temple tax (see 17:24-27). But it seems that having traders within the temple courts was a recent innovation. Jesus condemns this in 21:12-13 because...
   - this market-place crowded out space for prayer—hence Jesus' call for the temple to be "a house of prayer" (quoting Isaiah 56:7).
   - this monopoly led to extortionate prices—hence Jesus' condemnation of the temple as "a den of robbers" (quoting Jeremiah 7:11).

   But Jesus doesn't simply expel people from the temple. His ultimate goal is to welcome people into God's presence. Ordinarily the temple authorities excluded "the blind and the lame" from the temple, but in Jesus they find a welcome and healing (Matthew 21:14). And once again, Jesus welcomes the praise of little children. This theme of the self-righteous being excluded and the needy being welcomed continues throughout this section (v 31-32, 41, 43; 22:8-10). Jesus is enacting his declaration that "the last will be first, and the first will be last" (20:16; 19:30).

Explore More

- ***Read Malachi 3:1-2. Where have we seen a messenger preparing the way in Matthew?***
  Back in Matthew 11:7-11, Jesus said John the Baptist was the messenger promised by the prophet Malachi.
- ***What does Malachi say will happen next, after the messenger?***
  The Lord comes to his temple to refine and cleanse, smelting out the dross or washing out the dirt.
- ***How does this prophecy shed light on what is going on in these verses in Matthew 21?***
  This is what happens in Matthew 21 – 25. John has come as Malachi promised, and next Jesus comes as the Lord. In Matthew 21:1-11 Jesus enters Jerusalem as the King, coming to offer peace to rebels (as we saw in the previous chapter); in verses 12-17 Jesus enters the temple courts as the Lord, coming to refine and cleanse. This is followed by a sequence of conflicts in the temple courts in which Jesus exposes and condemns his opponents (21:23 – 23:36). Jesus is

setting in motion a chain of events that will ultimately lead to the destruction of the temple in AD 70, just as he predicts in 21:18-22, 23:37-39 and 24:15-21.

---

9. **The incident with the fig tree is an enacted parable about the temple (v 18-19). What is the message, do you think?**
Jesus had every reason to expect spiritual fruit from the temple and the religious system it represented. Indeed, like the leaves on the fig tree, the religious leaders declared their fruitfulness. But when Jesus came as the Lord to his temple, he found it barren (Matthew 3:8-10; 7:16-20; 12:33; 21:33-45). Their fig leaves are more like Adam's (Genesis 3:7), with their protestations of righteousness failing to hide their sin. So the cursing of the tree is an enacted curse on the temple (Matthew 21:43; 23:37-39; 24:15-21).

10. **Who do the two sons in the story represent?**
Jesus identifies the first son with tax collectors and prostitutes. At the start of their lives, they looked like people who refused to serve God, but now they're repenting of their sin and entering the kingdom through faith (v 31). The religious leaders are like the second son. They proclaimed their obedience but then refused to listen to God's prophet (v 32). The religious leaders saw themselves as custodians of the temple, but the house of prayer is being reassigned to repentant sinners.
If the religious leaders want to be "first" in the kingdom of God, what do they need to do? They need to become last: humble themselves, repent and believe in Jesus as God's Messiah (v 32).

11. **What warnings might there be for us in this section of Matthew?**
Encourage your group to share what has struck them. Valid warnings to take from this passage include warnings against self-righteousness; against outward religiosity that looks good to others but is devoid of spiritual fruit; and against excluding "the last" and the least from meeting Jesus.

- **What is the good news that we can take comfort in?**
If we are trusting in Jesus, we are not ultimately like the religious leaders in this passage; we're like the blind and the lame who have come to him for healing and the tax collectors and prostitutes who have entered the kingdom of God. We can take comfort in knowing that Jesus will not turn us away. Jesus himself is the ultimate obedient Son (Hebrews 10:5-7), and believing sinners are counted faithful in him.

12. **If we truly believe that "the last will be first, and the first will be last" in Jesus' kingdom, how might that shape how we do things in church life?**

    All are welcome in the church of Jesus—rich and poor, white and black, young and old, male and female, blue-collar and white-collar. But people must respond in the right way: that is, with faith and repentance. Are there ways in which wealth and status in worldly terms gain you privilege and status in the church? Are there barriers to "the blind and the lame"—or their equivalent—taking a full part in church life? What is it that is honoured and celebrated? Would a visitor to your church come away with the impression that you follow a Saviour who said, "The last will be first, and the first will be last"? These are sobering questions to ask of our church culture.

8

The Death of the King

Matthew 26:31-56; 27:32-54

The Big Idea

The disciples were faithless, but Jesus was faithful, all the way to the cross. His death unites us to God, reveals God to us, and gives us new life.

Summary

Since Jesus has finished teaching his disciples about the fall of the temple and being ready for his future return (26:1), the Gospel is now moving towards its climax, where "the Son of Man will be handed over to be crucified" (v 2).

Matthew devotes two full chapters to Jesus' passion. This session will focus on two particular episodes. The first is Gethsemane. Jesus tells the disciples they'll all desert him—literally, they'll "be scandalised" by him, the suffering Messiah (v 31; see 11:6). Peter protests, but Jesus says that Peter will disown him three times (26:33-35). This is the human condition. We've all betrayed God. Throughout human history, only one person has been consistently faithful to God, and humanity is about to execute him.

The problem, as Jesus tells Peter, is that "the spirit is willing, but the flesh is weak" (v 41). Jesus gives a twofold solution. First, he tells Peter to "watch and pray so that you will not fall into temptation" (v 41). But Peter doesn't watch and pray—instead, he sleeps (v 43). And later Peter does succumb to temptation (v 69-75, see Explore More). So Jesus gives a second solution to our weakness (see the first Getting Personal). He not only says to Peter to "watch and pray"; he also says to his Father, "May your will be done" (v 42). Like Peter, Jesus is willing. But unlike Peter, Jesus is willing to obey God even when it means draining to the dregs the cup of God's wrath (v 42).

In the second half of the session, we fast-forward to Matthew's account of the cross, where both the cost of Jesus' faithfulness and the wonderful consequences that flow to us through it are highlighted. In Matthew 27:45-54, Matthew describes Jesus' death from three perspectives with three matching consequences:

- *The cry and the curtain:* Jesus is abandoned by God (v 45-46) and thereby unites us to God (v 51).
- *The sponge and the centurion:* Jesus is misunderstood by humanity (v 47-49) and thereby reveals God to us (v 54).
- *The death and the resurrections:* Jesus gives up his life (v 50) and thereby gives life to us (v 52-53).

Ensure you leave time for reflection and prayers of praise and worship at the end of your time together.

Optional Extra

Set your group some challenges that will demonstrate the principle that "the spirit is willing but the flesh is weak". E.g. who can do the longest plank, go for the longest without blinking, or balance something on their head.

Guidance for Questions

1. **Share a time when you wanted to keep your word to someone but did not. What got in your way?**
Be ready with your own example if your group are struggling to say.

2. **How do the disciples rate their determination and faithfulness to Jesus (v 31-35)? What does Jesus think?**
Jesus tells the disciples they'll all desert him—literally, they'll "be scandalised" by him, the suffering Messiah (v 31; see 11:6). Peter protests, but Jesus says that Peter will disown him three times (26:33-35).

3. **Verses 36-46 present the disciples with an opportunity to prove their mettle! How do they fare?**
They do not fare well at all. Twice Jesus exhorts them to watch (or watch and pray, v 38, 41), and twice they fall asleep; the third time he doesn't even bother to wake them (v 44).

4. **Jesus is also being tested here. What is the temptation that he faces? How does he fare?**
The temptation—as Satan proposed in Matthew 4:1-11—is to bypass the cross and go straight to glory. Yet Jesus says to his Father, "May your will be done" (25:42). Unlike Peter, Jesus is willing to obey God even when it means draining to the dregs the cup of God's wrath (v 42; see Psalm 75:8 and Jeremiah 25:15-17). Here at last is a human being with human flesh who is faithful to God

in the power of the Spirit. He looks death, hell and wrath in the face, and he still says, "Yes" to God.

- **How do these verses underline the intensity of this moment for Jesus?**
We mustn't miss the anguish which Jesus endured to achieve this resolve. The prospect of death under God's wrath was overwhelming (v 38). Every fibre of his humanity shrank from it. Frederick Leahy suggests that Matthew says Jesus "began to be sorrowful and troubled" and was "overwhelmed with sorrow" (v 37-38, emphasis added) because this was the moment when Jesus first began to be forsaken by the Father (27:46): "God was placing [the cup] in the Saviour's hands and it carried the stench of hell." (*The Cross He Bore* (Banner of Truth, 1996), p. 5)

- **What would the consequences be for us if Jesus had said yes to this temptation in the garden?**
Jesus could have bypassed the cross. But then Jesus would not be "Jesus", the one whose name means "the Lord saves" (1:21). He would have come to glory without a people.

5. **How does Jesus show his control of the situation in these verses?**
   - Jesus stops his friends resisting his arrest (v 51-52).
   - Jesus rejects the option of calling on legions of angels (v 53).
   - Jesus says that what's happening is a fulfilment of the Scriptures (v 54-56).

- **Why is he willing to embrace death in this way?**
Jesus has wrestled in prayer and concluded, "Your will be done". Jesus is not the helpless victim of injustice; he's the active fulfiller of God's plan (v 54, 56). Jesus loves his Father and wants to glorify him. Jesus loves his people and wants to rescue us.

Explore More

- ***Read Matthew 26:69-75. How does Peter compare in this scene to the one in verses 31-35?***
Peter had been so full of passionate loyalty to Jesus. Now he is equally vehement in his denial of him. And it all ends in tears.

- ***What is significant about the number of times that Peter disowns Jesus? (Look back at verses 36-44.)***
It happens exactly as Jesus predicted. Also, three times Jesus had invited Peter to pray (v 38, 40-41, 43-44), but instead Peter had slept. Now Peter denies his Lord three times.

- ***Read Matthew 27:11-14. Compare these verses with Isaiah 53:7. What hope is there for weak and faithless Peter in this moment?***
At a key moment, Jesus is silent, to Pilate's great astonishment (27:11-14). Matthew is inserting a hypertext link back to the Suffering Servant of Isaiah. Matthew is again pointing to the meaning of the cross. There's hope for Peter because Jesus

is about to die in his place, bearing the penalty of sin that he deserves, as Isaiah 53:5 predicted. And there's hope for us in the same way.

- ***Imagine the early readers of Matthew's Gospel. They would have known Peter "the Rock" as a founding apostle of the church. What impact might reading this story of his failure have had on them, do you think?***
  Perhaps reading about his denial would have shocked them. Yet it demonstrates that there is a way back for anyone.

---

6. What should we do in light of our weakness, according to Jesus (v 41)? What does that mean, do you think?
"Watch and pray so that you will not fall into temptation. The spirit is willing, but the flesh is weak" (v 41). The exhortation is to watch and pray, and the reason is that the flesh is weak.
- To "watch" is to live as those who know the flesh is weak and so avoid situations when we might be tempted.
- To "pray" is to live as those who know it's God's Spirit who makes our spirits willing and so cry out for his help.

- **Are there specific ways you could build "watch and pray" into your life this week?**
  We may need to avoid watching certain TV programmes or reading certain books, if we know the temptation to lust is likely; we may need to avoid seeing particular friends in particular settings, or refuse to drink at all, if we suspect that the temptation to drink too much is likely to overwhelm us; we may need to leave our phone outside our bedroom if doom-scrolling before bed will lead us to fear and despair, and read a psalm instead.

- **How can we help one another?**
  One way we can do this is by holding each other accountable; you may each want to commit to an action step arising from the previous question, and then check in with each other about it when you next meet. Certainly, we can pray for each other in our battles, both as a group together and for one another throughout the week.

  NOTE: After this discussion, point your group to the first Getting Personal section in the Study Guide. This reflects on how the ultimate solution to our weakness is the obedience of Christ on our behalf.

7. What is the experience for Jesus described in verses 45-46?
Jesus is abandoned by God. At his baptism, heaven was opened and the Father declared his love (3:16-17). But now heaven is shut up against Jesus. Darkness is a sign of divine judgment. One of the Exodus plagues was darkness, and God had declared that one day in judgment, "I will make the sun go down at noon and darken the earth in broad daylight" (Amos 8:9; see also

Psalm 105:26-28). Yet here God is judging God; God the Son is being judged by God the Father. God treats his innocent Son as a guilty sinner so Jesus can pay the price of our sin.

- **What is the consequence for us, represented in verse 51?**
  Jesus unites us to God. The temple curtain screened off the Most Holy Place, keeping people from the dangerous presence of their holy God. The Most Holy Place was symbolically guarded by angels woven into the fabric of the curtain, just as angels had guarded the way back to Eden (Genesis 3:24; Exodus 26:30-33). It was shrouded in smoke from the altar of incense, just as God was hidden in cloud on Mount Sinai. Only the high priest could enter, only once a year, and only through sacrificial blood (Hebrews 9:7). Yet as Jesus died, the curtain of the temple was torn apart. The way to God is open. The old temple is replaced by Jesus himself as the place where God and humanity meet (Matthew 26:61; John 2:19-21). At the point when Jesus is most alone, he makes us family.

8. **What is the experience for Jesus described in verses 47-49?**
   Jesus is misunderstood by humanity. When Jesus calls out "Eli, Eli", some assume he's calling for Elijah (Matthew 27:47). It was thought that Elijah might return in the last times (see 3:4; 11:12-14; 17:10-13). So people assume this is a desperate, last-ditch plea of a man whose plans have gone horribly wrong.

- **What is the consequence for us, hinted at in verse 54?**
  Jesus reveals God to us. The centurion declares, "Surely he was the Son of God!". It's hard to know exactly what this man was thinking, but what's clear is that for Matthew, this declaration goes to the heart of what's happening. It looks as if Jesus is another failed messianic pretender: an idealist whose ideals have crumbled in the face of brute force. But Matthew says, *That's not what's happening.* Instead, the cross is a revelation of God. The proof that Jesus is God comes not through the fireworks of a mighty miracle but in the self-giving love of the cross. Only God is capable of such love.

9. **What is the experience for Jesus described in verse 50?**
   Jesus gives up his life. Jesus experiences the ultimate enemy of humankind: death itself.

- **What is the consequence for us, previewed in verses 52-53?**
  Jesus gives life to us. As Jesus died, "the earth shook ... and the tombs broke open", and Matthew speaks of dead people coming back to life. Matthew calls them "holy people". These were old-covenant believers. We don't know what happened to them afterwards—probably they went back to the grave to await the final resurrection. They were simply a

foretaste of what is yet to come. While the tombs broke open as Jesus died, the bodies were raised only "after Jesus' resurrection" on the first Easter Sunday (v 53). So, why does Matthew include their resurrection here, rather than in chapter 28, when it actually took place? Matthew 27:51 begins, "At that moment": Jesus gave up his life, and at that moment, tombs broke open. Matthew wants us to see cause and effect. Jesus gives up his life, and as a result, we receive our life.

10. **How does what we've read help us when...**
    - **we feel the weight of guilt for our sin?**
      The tearing of the temple curtain shows that as humanity's rebellion reaches its dark, twisted climax, God flings open his arms to embrace us in his love. Jesus loved us when our hatred plunged as deep as it could go. Sometimes, when we feel the weight of sin, we doubt whether anyone can love us. But "God demonstrates his own love for us in this: while we were still sinners, Christ died for us" (Romans 5:8). If Jesus loved you as they drove nails into his wrists, then he loves you now.
    - **we are suffering and feel abandoned by God?**
      Sometimes in our pain, we cry out, "Why me? Why are you letting this happen? My God, why have you forsaken me?" All those cries were echoed by Jesus as he hung on the tree. Those cries of confusion and pain have become part of the story of Jesus. God himself, in the person of his Son, has experienced what it is to feel forsaken by God (Hebrews 4:15). He has not abandoned us; he loves us. It was not the nails that kept Jesus on the cross; what held Jesus on the cross was love.

9

The King Lives

Matthew 28:1-10, 16-20

The Big Idea

We need not fear because Jesus has risen, and therefore he is Lord; Jesus is Lord, and therefore he claims the nations; Jesus claims the nations, and therefore he sends us to call people to repentance.

Summary

The first half of this session looks at Matthew's account of the resurrection in 28:1-11. Matthew is at pains to show us that on the first Easter Sunday, a human being who had died came back to life again: a real death followed by a real resurrection (see Explore More). We may find the resurrection of Jesus hard to believe because it's not the sort of thing that happens in a world under the dominion of death (Romans 5:12, 17). But the resurrection of Jesus is the beginning of a new world—indicated by the two "time markers" at the start of Matthew 28:1 ("at dawn on the first day of the week").

The message of the resurrection is not *Anything is possible in this world. Even when things seem hopeless, hope might yet emerge.* Instead, in the resurrection God is saying, "Behold, I am making all things new" (Revelation 21:5, ESV; see Isaiah 43:19; 65:17). Jesus is "the firstborn from among the dead"—the first person to be birthed out of the grave into a new life in a new world (Colossians 1:18).

Christ's resurrection is witnessed by two women called Mary (one of whom may be his mother), who have two resurrection encounters: with an angel and with Jesus. In both cases, the first words they hear are "Do not be afraid" (Matthew 28:5, 10). This is the message of the resurrection: Jesus has risen to end our fear. We don't need to fear sin, for the crucified one is risen. And we don't need to fear people, for the rejected one is risen.

The second half of the session focuses on the Great Commission, in verses 16-20. This happens in Galilee, a location associated with the Gentiles (see 4:12-17 and Isaiah 9:1-7). We know from the other Gospels that Jesus appeared to the disciples in Jerusalem—on Easter Sunday and then again a week later (John 20:19, 26). But Matthew leaves all of this out to focus on Galilee and amplify his message: the fulfilment of the resurrection is the worship of the nations. This is seen in the words of the Great Commission, when the risen Jesus, the one with "all authority", sends his disciples to "all nations" to teach "everything" (literally "all the things") Jesus has commanded them. The logic is...

- Jesus has risen, and therefore he is Lord.
- Jesus is Lord, and therefore he claims the nations.

- Jesus claims the nations, and therefore he sends us to call people to repentance.

As we do so, we can be assured of Jesus' presence with us by his Spirit, "to the very end of the age" (Matthew 28:20).

Optional Extra

If members of your group are unfamiliar with the historical evidence for the resurrection, you could watch a short video after question 5 such as this one, featuring the author Lee Strobel: www.youtube.com/watch?v=FT4Cj-Pi4m0.

If you didn't have time for extended prayer for mission partners as part of Session 4 (see Optional Extra, p. 83), you could do that at the end of this study. (Or do it again!)

Guidance for Questions

1. **What have been some of the recurring themes you've noticed as we've studied Matthew's Gospel?**
   This is an opportunity to reflect on the journey we've been on. It will also tee up some of the themes we'll see again in this study. These include the first being last and the last being first; Jesus' authority and his identity as the Christ/Messiah; and Jesus' mission beyond the Jewish people to the nations/Gentiles. But there are many more themes than that to spot in this final chapter of Matthew.

2. **Put yourself in Mary Magdalene and the other Mary's shoes for a moment. What else have they witnessed in the past three days (see 27:55-56, 59-61)?**
   They have watched their friend Jesus, whom they have followed all the way "from Galilee", be brutally executed. (In fact, "the other Mary" may have been Jesus' mother). And they have watched him be buried in a tomb with a big stone over its entrance.
   - **What do you think they were expecting to find on that Sunday morning? What did they see instead?**
   No doubt they were expecting to find the tomb as they had left it 36 hours earlier. Instead they experience an earthquake, witness an angel surrounded by the passed-out guards, hear that Jesus has risen and then meet him themselves.

3. **Why might it be significant that it's two women who play a key part in the action on this momentous morning?**
   All the way through the passion story, the action has involved men. The women stand on the periphery with no role and no voice (27:55-56, 61). But not on Easter Sunday! In Matthew's resurrection account, men are notable by their absence. It's women who come to the tomb, witness the earthquake, are spoken to by the angel, first meet the risen Christ and are given a job to do (28:1-2, 5-10). The kingdom of Christ turns the priorities and verdicts of this world upside down because the one who was rejected has been exalted. Jesus

is the ultimate "nobody" who turns out to be the ultimate somebody.

4. **Matthew doesn't usually give precise indicators of time in his Gospel, but he begins his resurrection account with two (28:1). What might they tell us about what the resurrection represents? (Hint: Part of it has something to do with the creation account in Genesis 1!)**
   Matthew tells us it was "after the Sabbath" and "at dawn on the first day" (Matthew 28:1). The old creation took place over seven days (culminating in the Sabbath on day seven), and this is the age in which we currently live. But Easter Sunday takes place "after" the Sabbath day. Easter is the beginning of a new work of creation—a renewed humanity living in a renewed world. And the resurrection takes place "at dawn" because the resurrection is itself a "dawn"—of a new age. The resurrection of Jesus is just the beginning; but the beginning has begun.

5. **The women have two encounters: one with an angel and one with Jesus. What are they told in both cases (v 5, 10)? Why might that reassurance have been necessary?!**
   In both cases, among the first words the women hear are "Do not be afraid" (v 5, 10). The supernatural nature of the events would have been reason enough for fear. They might also have been afraid that Jesus would be angry at the disciples' failure on the day of his death. Moreover, in the Old Testament, earthquakes were associated with "the day of the LORD", when he was going to come in judgment (Joel 2:1, 10-11; Haggai 2:6-7). So, the women might be expecting fearful words of condemnation from Jesus. Instead, they hear these wonderful words of reassurance.

6. **Why does the resurrection mean we don't need to fear sin?**
   The angel could simply have said, "I know that you are looking for Jesus ... He's not here; he has risen." But he adds, "who was crucified" (v 5-6). This is not merely another miracle, like the raising of the synagogue ruler's daughter in 9:18-26. Jesus died under the judgment of God, and he could only rise if that judgment had been satisfied. And it has! The resurrection is God's declaration that the price is paid. It's not Jesus the good man who has risen—that would mean hope only for those as good as Jesus. It's Jesus the God-forsaken man who has risen—and that brings hope for sinners.

- **Why does the resurrection mean we don't need to fear people?**
  This connects with the answer to question 3 about the women. The kingdom of Christ turns the priorities and verdicts of this world upside down because the one who was rejected has been exalted. The men of chapter 27 passed their verdict on Christ: they dismissed him as a religious blasphemer and a political rebel. But

the resurrection is *God's* verdict. The verdict of humanity is overturned in the heavenly court of appeal.

Still today the people of Christ—men and women—are mocked and ridiculed, and Christian beliefs and ethics are often marginalised. But the verdict of the world has been overturned in heaven, and one day it will be reversed on earth. "Many who are first will be last, and many who are last will be first" (19:30; 20:16).

Explore More

- ***Read Matthew 27:57-66; 28:11-15. What details does Matthew provide us with to counter the claims that...***
- ***Jesus merely fainted on the cross and revived in the tomb?***
  We get a sense of the care with which Joseph handles the body of Jesus: taking it, wrapping it, placing it. He would have noticed if Jesus was still breathing. More significantly, Jesus didn't "dip" into death. He was in the tomb for two nights and three days. Whatever happened on Easter Sunday, it wasn't a resuscitation. Jesus was dead and buried.

- ***Jesus' body was stolen—the resurrection was a hoax?***
  Fearing the disciples might steal the body, the religious leaders persuade Pilate to make the tomb secure (Matthew 27:63-64). The guards prevent anyone getting in, and the seal prevents anyone getting out. Yet having made theft impossible, this is the explanation of the empty tomb that is then proposed by the religious leaders—even though it's the one explanation they know cannot be true (28:11-15).

- ***Why is it important that what happened on the first Easter Sunday was a real resurrection?***
  It's not simply that the ideals of Jesus live on. We sometimes talk of people living on in our memories or their example continuing to inspire, but the resurrection of Jesus was so much more than this. It's the beginning of a new world. In the resurrection God is saying, "Behold, I am making all things new" (Revelation 21:5, ESV; see Isaiah 43:19; 65:17). Jesus is "the firstborn from among the dead"—the first person to be birthed out of the grave into a new life in a new world (Colossians 1:18), of which we too can be part.

- ***What possibility do the chief priests fail to consider in 28:12? What does that tell us about the nature of their unbelief, do you think?***
  The chief priests don't pause for a moment to consider that the empty tomb might mean Jesus is who he said he was. In 27:42 the Pharisees promise to believe Jesus if he comes down from the cross. But even when Jesus steps from the tomb, they refuse to believe. That's because the root of unbelief doesn't lie in the intellect but in the heart. The real problem is that if the resurrection is

for real, it means there's a God whom we should obey, and it means Jesus is his Son. But people don't want to obey God or acknowledge their need of Jesus, so it's more "convenient" not to believe.

---

7. **Jesus says that "all authority" has been given to him (v 18). How have we seen him display his complete authority already in Matthew's Gospel?**
   Jesus came as the Messiah to re-establish God's kingdom on earth. He came with royal authority to heal the sick, feed the hungry, liberate the possessed and preach good news. This is evident all over Matthew's Gospel, but we especially saw it in study 4 with the calming of the storm, restoration of two demon-possessed men and the forgiving and healing of the paralysed man (8:23 – 9:8).

- **What has changed (and what is about to change) at this point? (See 26:64 and Acts 1:9-11.)**
  Jesus' authority was resisted and rejected. In the end we crucified our King. But now Jesus has risen and is about to ascend into heaven. Jesus will pass through the clouds to receive the authority of God and the praise of heaven (26:64; Daniel 7:13-14). Jesus' ascension is like a coronation. Jesus is about to ascend into heaven to be worshipped by angels, and Matthew gives us a little preview of all this in Matthew 28:16-17 as Jesus ascends a mountain to be worshipped by disciples.

- **What appropriate response to Jesus' authority do we see in Matthew 28:17 (and also verse 9)?**
  The disciples worship him. If Jesus is God's King, then we must bow before him. Every area of life is to be governed by his rule.

8. **What connection is there between Jesus' command in verse 19 and his statement in verse 18?**
   Matthew 28:19 begins, "Therefore". The *Great Commission* is the logic of the *great enthronement* in verse 18. It's because Jesus has received authority over all nations that he sends us to all nations. The logic is there in the word "all" (v 19). Jesus is given "all authority"; Jesus sends us to "all nations"; we are to teach "everything" (literally "*all* the things") Jesus has commanded us.

9. **Why is this a fitting end to Matthew's Gospel, given what we've read so far?**
   All the way through his Gospel, Matthew has pointed us forward to the mission to the Gentiles, or nations. Jesus is the son of Abraham who will bless the nations (1:1; Genesis 12:1-3). At his birth, the Magi bring the worship of the nations (Matthew 2:1-12). And so it goes on (3:8-9; 8:11; 10:18; 11:20-24; 24:14).

   Even the structure of Matthew puts the focus on our mission. As we've seen, Matthew's Gospel is divided into five sections, each of which ends, "When Jesus had finished saying these things" (7:28; 11:1; 13:53; 19:1; 26:1). But what happens when the story reaches its climax with the death and resurrection of Jesus? Instead of more teaching from Jesus, we find Jesus commissioning us, his church, to teach (28:19).

10. **It's a big mission! What reassurance does Jesus give his disciples?**
    Matthew ends his Gospel with Jesus saying, "And surely I am with you always, to the very end of the age" (28:20). It's literally "all the days"—a fourth "all" to add to all authority, all nations, and all things. Jesus was about to ascend into heaven, and so he'd be physically absent. But Jesus would be with them through the Holy Spirit.

11. **Global mission is not a niche interest for Christians. We're all called to play our part. What does that already look like you (as an individual and as part of your church)? How would you like it to look in the future?**
    It might mean praying each day for missionaries you know, financially supporting their work or signing up for prayer news. Or today the risen Christ might be calling some in your group to leave their home and take the good news to another nation.

12. **How do Jesus' words in verses 18-19 challenge you?**
    Jesus has received "all authority". He is Lord of our work, our marriage, our wallet, our leisure, our service, our family. The burden of his rule is light, for he's a liberating King who reigns in love (11:30). But nevertheless, he is our King, and he must be obeyed.

- **How do they bring you comfort?**
  Paul writes, "God placed all things under his feet and appointed him to be head over everything for the church, which is his body" (Ephesians 1:22-23). Christ rules for the sake of the body to which he is intimately joined in love, like a husband to his wife (5:25-33). Jesus exercises his authority to protect you, guide you, keep you and ultimately lead you home to glory. You're safe in the hands of the one who holds the world in his hands.

- **How do they inspire your courage?**
  Jesus is with us by his Spirit. He's with us in our homes, with all the challenges which that involves. He's with us in the workplace when our faith is being mocked. He's with us when we serve the needy (25:34-40). Whatever problems we're facing, we can know this: Christ is risen. He's alive. And he's with you always, to the very end. He is your Immanuel.